The North as Home:

Proceedings from the Nordic Research Network 2017

eds. Heidi Synnøve Djuve, Stefan Drechsler,
Beñat Elortza Larrea and Deniz Cem Gülen

Norvik Press
2019

© 2019 Christian Cooijmans, Jan D. Cox, Andrea Freund, Isabelle Gapp, Blake Middleton, Victoria Ralph, Aya Shimano-Bardai, Ruairidh Tarvet, Miriam Tveit.

Norvik Press Series C: Student Writing no. 4

A catalogue record for this book is available from the British Library.

ISBN: 978-1-909408-54-8

Norvik Press
Department of Scandinavian Studies
University College London
Gower Street
London WC1E 6BT
United Kingdom
Website: www.norvikpress.com
E-mail address: norvik.press@ucl.ac.uk

Managing editors: Elettra Carbone, Sarah Death, Janet Garton, C. Claire Thomson.

Cover image: Detail of woodcut made by Gerhard Munthe as found in Anne Holtsmark and Didrik Arup Seip (1934) (eds.), *Snorres Kongesagaer, Annet Bind*. Oslo: Gyldendal Forlag, p. 213. All rights reserved.
Cover design and layout: Essi Viitanen

This volume was made possible with financial support from the University of Aberdeen Development Trust Experience Fund.

Contents

Acknowledgements — 5

Introduction — 7

HISTORICAL HOMES

**An Adversary for the Ages:
The Late Medieval Historiography of Viking Endeavour across the Low Countries.
A Preliminary Survey** — 12
Christian Cooijmans

European Trade Networks in the Medieval High North — 32
Miriam Tveit

Runes in Orkney: Making a Diaspora a Home? — 50
Andrea Freund

VISUAL HOMES

Skagen: A Utopia of the North? — 70
Jan D. Cox

**A Swedish Landscape?
Nature and Identity in the Paintings of Gustav Fjæstad and Helmer Osslund** — 94
Isabelle Gapp

PRESENT HOMES

Nordic Sound Art: Aspects of an Artistic Collectivity   110
Aya Shimano-Bardai

Mapping out Identity in the German-Danish
Borderlands: New Perspectives on Hybridising
Identity in Minority Communities   122
Ruairidh Tarvet

MYTHOLOGICAL HOMES

Which Way to Jǫtunheimar?
A Study of the Multiple Realms of the Jǫtnar   142
Blake Middleton

A Haunted Home on a Northern Moor in
Selma Lagerlöf's *Stenkumlet*   160
Victoria Ralph

Notes on contributors   180

Acknowledgements

The editors are very grateful to all the contributors to this book for sharing their intriguing research on a great variety of aspects of home in the northern hemisphere.

We would like to thank the University of Aberdeen Development Trust Experience Fund. This volume would not have been possible without its generous financial support. Furthermore, we would like to thank Dr Mary Pryor from the University of Aberdeen, as well as Norvik Press, especially Dr Claire Thomson and Dr Essi Viitanen, for their work on the editing and production of this book. Finally, as this volume is the outcome of the 7th Nordic Research Network Conference hosted by the Centre for Scandinavian Studies and the Department of Archaeology at University of Aberdeen on 24-25th August 2017, we would like to thank the other conference organisers Pam Correy, Michael Frost, Ann Sølvia Lydersen Jacobsen and Keith Ruiter for their time and efforts.

Introduction

This volume stems from the Nordic Research Network (NRN) 2017 Conference, which was the fifth event organised under the banner of the NRN since 2010. The conference was held for two days at the University of Aberdeen on 24-25 August 2017. As at previous events, it hosted a successful forum for new and innovative research in the humanities with a diverse range of methodologies across the various disciplines dedicated to Nordic research in the broadest sense. With thirty-two presenters, four keynote speakers, a roundtable discussion and a well-attended workshop by Norvik Press and Brepols Publishers on academic publishing, the NRN 2017 Conference was one of the largest conferences held in the UK dedicated to Nordic research.

Following the increased research interest in regional aspects of Nordic life during recent decades, this book addresses selected aspects of the meaning of 'home' in the north.[1] Definitions, connotations and contexts of the term have been discussed in the humanities for in a long time, and a wide variety of interpretations are the subject of vigorous research today.[2] Accordingly, the aim of this volume is to present important current approaches in the humanities, all under the umbrella of what can be classified as 'home' in the arts, sociology, literature and history of the northernmost reaches of the European continent. In particular, this volume seeks to provide new interdisciplinary research and knowledge on topics relating to textual, material, archaeological, visual and musical sources and concepts of 'home'.

The first section of this volume begins with a number of approaches to three noteworthy regions of early Medieval northern Europe. Accordingly, it is asked how they changed throughout the centuries as different settling and trading activities altered the local, political, and social landscapes. Opening with an encounter on Viking history in the Low Countries, Christian

Cooijmans analyses late medieval historiographical descriptions of Viking activity in previous centuries. The following chapter by Miriam Tveit discusses the European dimensions of trade in the northern parts of Norway during the High and Late Medieval times. Finally, Andrea Freund investigates whether the evidence of Runic inscriptions in Orkney speaks for a Viking diaspora during the High Middle Ages and beyond. The second section explores the social background to visual representations of Scandinavian landscapes and societies in the late nineteenth century, and how they may be connected with the representations of 'home' created by the artists. Jan Cox discusses the artist colony at the northern Jutish town of Skagen, and how this artist colony came to be in close contact with the local notable families of the area, as well as with the further population of northern Jutland. Isabelle Gapp, meanwhile, sheds light on the Swedish painters Gustav Fjærstad and Helmer Osslund, and how their depictions of Swedish landscape can be understood as part of a wider Nordic or even northern circumpolar art.

The penultimate section illuminates two approaches to the ideas of homes in the present. Aya Shimano-Bardai's contribution presents a range of artistic aspects shared by the members of the Nordic Sound Art movement, with particular focus given to certain aspects of the artistic collectivity such as equal philosophies, workshops and approaches to sound and recording. Ruairidh Tarvet presents new perspectives on the German-Danish borderlands from the views of minority communities in the neighbouring countries both in history and today.

The final part of this book provides two approaches to mythological homes as found in two forms of Nordic literature and mythology. Blake Middleton explores the realms of Old Norse Jǫtnar and their location in pre-Christian Scandinavian mythology. Victoria Ralph shines light on the short story *Stenkumlet* by Swedish literature Nobel laureate Selma Lagerlöf, in which an Old Norse-inspired story of a Swedish heathen place is retold.

All the contributions in this volume present new and innovative approaches to concepts of 'home' in the north. While creating this book, we have found the contributions to be most enjoyable to work with, and it is our hope that the readership will have a similarly enjoyable experience while exploring these nine approaches to a 'home' in the north. This book is the third in the series published by Norvik Press under the banner of the NRN, following the previous edited volumes, titled *Illuminating the North* by Broomé et al (2014) and *Beyond Borealism: New Perspectives on the North* by Giles et al (2016). Encompassing a similarly wide variety of topics, this volume invites the reader to inspiring discussion.

On behalf of the editorial team,
Stefan Drechsler
Greifswald, spring 2019

Endnotes

[1] According to the Oxford English Dictionary, the term 'home' derives from a variety of Germanic words such as Old English hām, German heim and Dutch heem, and, ultimately, Indo-Germanic k̂ei. Similar to modern use, k̂ei provides a wide semantic field of the word with examples such as 'familiar, settling', or simply 'home' or 'place'. See Pokorny (1989, 539-540) for the term and its various meanings.

[2] See Mallet (2004, with further references) for a short review on recent scholarship on the meaning, connotation and context of 'home' in various disciplines in the humanities such as sociology, history and philosophy.

References

Broomé, A., Chow, P.-S., Smalley, N., Taylor, L., Viitanen, E. (eds.) (2014). *Illuminating the North: Proceedings from the Nordic Research Network 2013*. London: Norvik Press.

Giles, I., Chapot, L., Cooijmans, C., Foster, R., Tesio, B. (eds.) (2016). *Beyond Borealism: New Perspectives on the North*. London: Norvik Press.

Mallet, S. (2004). 'Understanding home: a critical review of the literature', *The Sociological Review*, 52(1), pp. 62-89.

Pokorny, J. (1994). *Indogermanisches etymologisches Wörterbuch*. Dritte Auflage. Vol. 1. Bern: Francke.

HISTORICAL HOMES

An Adversary for the Ages: The Late Medieval Historiography of Viking Endeavour across the Low Countries.
A Preliminary Survey

Christian Cooijmans

Introduction

[...] les Liegois l'ont entrepris à enwaleir [...]. Mains vos deveis savoir que al avaleir furent là troveis des corps d'hommes mors qui tenoient X pies ou XII de hault, et les plus petis si tenoient IX pies; et avoient leurs espeez deleis eaux, toutes enrunies et brisies et pouries. Li peuple enfuit tout espawenteis, car ilh ne savoit dont ilhs venoient là ne queis gens ch'estoient [...]; mains chu furent Normans qui furent là ochis par l'evesque Franque de Liège [...]. (Bormans 1880: 311).

(The people of Liège endeavoured to build a wall [...]. But you should know that, whilst digging, the bodies of dead men were found, which were ten or twelve feet tall, and the smallest were nine feet; and they had their swords upon them, all rusted and broken and decayed. The crowd fled in distress, because they did not know where these people came from or who they were [...]; these, however, were the Northmen who were killed by Bishop Franco of Liège [...].)[1]

This conspicuous passage is found in the *Myreur des histors* ('Mirror of History'), a late fourteenth-century chronicle by Jean des Preis (styled d'Outremeuse), detailing the discovery of human remains in his native Liège during the year 1326. The unusually tall stature of the armed skeletons led the author to conclude that these were no ordinary men, but the very Northmen whose purported tenth-century attack on the city he had recounted earlier on in his work (Bormans 1877: 85-86). For Jean and many of his contemporaries, a historical awareness of local and regional viking[2] activity relied on the transmission of a highly diverse corpus of narrative sources – compiled, transcribed, and reinterpreted over the course of several centuries. In Liège itself, for example, authors may have been conversant with the early thirteenth-century *Chronica pontificum Leodiensium*, which contains the following passage:

> Et abbaciam S[anc]ti Petri a Beato Huberto in Leodio fundatam vastaverunt. Fratres in ea existentes perimerunt cunctamque civitatem destruxerunt, ecclesiam totam combusserunt, feretro Beati Lamberti ab igne intacto remanente pariter et illeso. (Franz 1882: 43).

> (And the abbey of St. Peter in Liège, founded by the blessed Hubert, was laid waste. The brothers living there were killed, and they destroyed the entire city and burnt down the whole church, the coffin of the blessed Lambert remaining untouched and unharmed by the fire.)

No more than a few decades later, another author from Liège, Gilles d'Orval, recounted the same viking attack in much greater detail:

> Et quod abbatia Sancti Petri in Leodio a beato Huberto fundata, tunc vastata sit, innuitur ex eo quod monachorum

> capita, qui ab eis martyrizati sunt, clavis ferreis et capitalibus confixa inventa sunt in pilariis et in cripta eiusdem ecclesie tumulata. [...] Cum etiam itidem Normanni cunctam civitatem vastarent, feretrum beati Lamberti [...] infringer volentes, divinitus timore perculsi eum contingere non potuerunt, et sic tristes recedentes [...]. (Heller 1880: 49).

> (And the abbey of St. Peter in Liège, founded by the blessed Hubert, was then laid waste, [and] it is suggested that the heads of the monks, those who were martyred, were found fastened to its columns with iron nails and buried in the tomb of the same church. [...] When those Northmen also wished to lay waste to all of the city, determined to break the coffin of the blessed Lambert, [...] they were not able to touch him, having been struck with the fear of God, and so these wretched men withdrew [...].)

Regardless of whether the second passage is based on the first or both follow a joint base text, a narrative link between the two texts is in evidence. Since no known records from the Viking Age itself impart the above-mentioned events so explicitly, later accounts like these seem to represent a gradual process of textual embellishment, produced by the imagination of consecutive generations of intermediate authorship.[3]

Conceivably acquainted with these scenes of brutality, Jean's rationale for the imposing bodies to have belonged to malevolent vikings becomes a much more fathomable premise. Knowingly or not, he himself contributed to this ongoing process of narrative transmission, by which the distant vikings and their actions – both real and imagined – were embedded into an expanding and evolving historical consciousness. This chapter, representing a preliminary study, endeavours to explore how and why late medieval historians throughout the Low Countries recollected, represented, and repurposed the viking phenomenon. Whereas many of the works under consideration have already been subject to extensive scholarly scrutiny (e.g. Burgers 1999; Mol and Smithuis 2008; Driel 2012), the particular role played by vikings within them has only seldom been highlighted.

The Viking Age Low Countries

Before examining its later medieval portrayal, it is warranted to provide a brief outline of the documented and otherwise attested Scandinavian presence across the region during the Viking Age itself. The Low Countries, broadly corresponding to the territories of the present-day Netherlands, Belgium, and Luxembourg, encompass the lower basins of the Rivers Rhine, Meuse, and Scheldt. By the eighth century, this area had been wholly incorporated into the Frankish realm under the auspices of the Carolingian dynasty (Milis 2006: 12-15; Bachrach 2001: 249). At this time, economic and cultural exchanges with Scandinavia were already well-established, as intrepid merchants, missionaries, and other migrants continued to make their way overseas in ever-increasing volumes (Loveluck 2013: 195-196; Lebecq 2012: 15-16, 21).

Formal Franco-Scandinavian relations were less amicable, however, as political tensions between Charlemagne and the Danish monarchy culminated in a large-scale military incursion along the Frisian coast in 810, detailed by contemporary sources like the *Annales regni Francorum* (Kurze 1895: 131). More recurrent forays were reported during the 830s, when commercial centres like Domburg-*Walichrum* and Dorestad became principal targets of viking antagonism, the latter being assailed at least nine times over the course of three decades (Waitz 1883: 9, 11-13, 35, 61; Pertz 1829b: 228). As Scandinavian aggressors grew in confidence and capability, their operations began to move increasingly inland, with prominent political nuclei like Nijmegen, Cologne, and even Aachen – the erstwhile heart of Carolingian courtly life

– being besieged during the 880s (Kurze 1891: 96-97; Waitz 1883: 153). Eventually, a combination of preventative and remedial countermeasures, including the payment of tributes, granting of (landed) benefices, and construction of fortifications, allowed Frankish elites to curb this Scandinavian aggression, which had been all but extinguished across the region by the early tenth century.

Cultures of writing

For several subsequent centuries, the regional exploits of these bygone viking hosts seem to have reverberated across the cultural memory of the Low Countries, even as the territory itself remained embroiled in the ongoing geopolitical contentions of the Kingdom of France, the Holy Roman Empire, and the emergent Duchy of Burgundy (Prevenier 2000). During the later Middle Ages, a diverse culture of writing blossomed throughout this relatively small region, accelerated by an increasingly literate urban middle class, which depended on the written word for the provision and consumption of numerous administrative and intellectual services and pastimes (Pleij 2009: 63; Schryver 1997: 132). This was a society able to recognise and recontextualise its own history, progressively employing the vernaculars of Dutch and French alongside the Latin which had monopolised prior written discourse (Oostrom 2009: 37; Schryver 1997: 132).

Across the region, the appropriation of historical narratives began to play a significant role in the reinforcement of collective identities, including those of prominent dynasties, monastic houses, and wider urban or provincial communities as a whole. For groups like these, reimagining the past served to establish precedent, to legitimise and glorify political and ecclesiastical authority, and – conversely – to disenfranchise any perceived opposition (Schryver 1997: 161, 174-175; Prevenier and Blockmans 1986: 219-220; Schneidmüller 2002).[4] In light of these rationales, a large share of regional late medieval chronicles may be more effectively examined as works of contemporary political proselytism than as depictions of historical reality. Meanwhile, genre conventions were also becoming increasingly intermingled, making it more and more difficult – at times even counterproductive – to ascribe contemporary narratives to fixed textual categories (Ebels-Hoving 1987: 227-228; Schryver 1997: 161). Regional annals, for example, may have been endowed with hagiographical elements, whilst dynastic chronicles could contain features of chivalric romance, and so forth. Finally, as seen above, histories like these borrowed heavily from one another, often copying entire sections to the letter.

As hundreds of narrative works like these are recognised to have been produced within the geographical reach of the present-day Netherlands alone (Carasso-Kok 1981), this chapter will limit itself to a number of prolific late medieval examples in exploring the role vikings continued to play in the authorial consciousness of this post-viking era.

Vikings and their portrayal

Throughout the late medieval Low Countries, the viking phenomenon continued to receive a marked amount of authorial attention. Despite its drawn-out narrative transmission, however, some elements of this Scandinavian endeavour remain largely faithful to the ninth-century source material. A straightforward example is seen in descriptions of the 881 viking attack on Aachen, which was recorded as follows by the contemporary *Annales Fuldenses*:

> At illi instaurato exercitu et amplificato numero equitum plurima loca in regione regis nostri vastaverunt, [...] monasteria, id est Prumiam, Indam, Stabulaus, Malmundarium

et Aquense palatium, ubi in capella regis equis suis stabulum fecerunt. (Kurze 1891: 96-97).

(But they renewed their army and increased the number of horsemen and pillaged many places in the lands of our king: [...] the monasteries of Prüm, Cornelimünster, Stavelot, Malmedy, and the palace of Aachen, where they used the king's chapel as a stable for their horses.) (Reuter 1992: 90).

This latter indignation – in particular – outlived the Carolingian period, and was recounted by historians like Sigebert of Gembloux during the early twelfth century: '[...] Aquis in palatio equos stabulantes, oppidum et palatium incendunt [...]' (Pertz 1844: 343) (Horses were stabled in the palace of Aachen, and the town and palace were set aflame). A century later, Vincent of Beauvais, in producing his encyclopaedic *Speculum maius* ('The Great Mirror'), cited Sigebert as one of his sources, copying the above passage almost verbatim (Benedictines of St. Vaast 1624: 978). His work was then promptly translated into several vernaculars, of which a well-known Middle Dutch adaptation – in verse – was realised by Jacob van Maerlant during the 1280s:

> Aken wonnen si die stede,
> Ende indes keysers pallayse mede
> Hebben si ghestallet hare paerde
> Den Roemscen rike teere onwaerde.
> (Utenbroeke and Velthem 1863: 238).

(They conquered the city of Aachen,
And likewise in the emperor's palace
Did they stable their horses
Unworthy of the Roman empire's honour.)

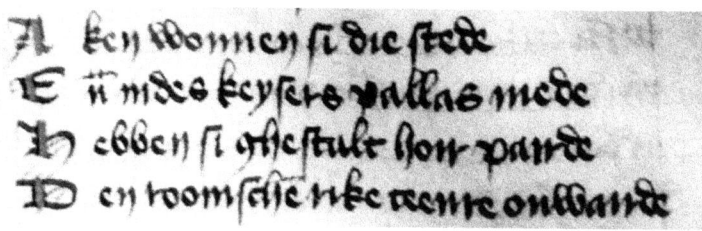

Fig. 1: Detail from the early fifteenth-century Haagse Handschift *('the Hague Manuscript') of Claes Heynensoon, herald at the court of Holland. The Hague, National Library of the Netherlands, MS 131 G 37 fol. 25ra31-34. Photo: Christian Cooijmans.*

This excerpt was subsequently reproduced by various authors throughout the fourteenth and fifteenth centuries, including Claes Heynensoon, the Bavarian herald at the early fifteenth-century court of Holland (Verbij-Schillings 1999: 139 – see also Fig. 1).

Although by no means a comprehensive chronology, these successive examples demonstrate the consistency with which some of these passages were handed down over the course of half a millennium or more. This was hardly typical, however, as many late medieval chroniclers instead sought to depict vikings in various anachronistic or out-of-place scenarios, deliberately or otherwise.

An effective case study is presented by the coastal County of Holland, whose progenitor was identified by numerous late medieval chroniclers as Count Theoderic, or Dirk. Although credited with a variety of virtuous deeds, Dirk's encounters with regionally operative vikings seem to rank among his most celebrated achievements, as manifest – for example – in Johannes de Beke's mid-fourteenth-century *Chronographia*, composed at Egmond Abbey: '[...] Theodricus et sua posteritas eandem dicionem feodali iure possiderunt ac atroces Danos de finibus Romani regni potentissime profugarent' (Bruch 1973: 55)

(Dirk and his descendants held this same lordship [Holland] as a rightful benefice, and firmly expelled the cruel Danes from the borders of the Roman realm). Tracing its institutional roots to the tenures of the count and his immediate successors, the praise bestowed on Dirk by the community of Egmond should come as no great surprise (Mostert 1993: 16). But corresponding accolades also arose elsewhere, including the anonymous late fifteenth-century *Kattendijke-kroniek*, of presumed secular origin (Tilmans 1998: 181):

> Dirck, die eerste also ghenoemt, [...] was die eerste graef van Hollant ende Zelant ende heer van Vrieslant totter Louwers toe, xxxviii jaer lanck. [...] Hij keerde die Denen ende heyden stoutelicken uut sijnen lande. (Tilmans 2005: 185).
>
> (Dirk, first of his name, [...] was the first count of Holland and Zeeland and lord of Frisia up to the [River] Lauwers, for thirty-eight years. [...] He boldly drove the Danes and heathens from his land.)

Despite these retrospective attributions, very few details about Dirk survive from the Viking Age itself. It is nevertheless clear that his inauguration as count would have taken place sometime during the early tenth century, a time when viking endeavour had already practically disappeared from the region (Bruch 1986: 3). Hence, his illustrious suppression of these Scandinavian interlopers is likely to be an anachronism – a foundational myth contrived to legitimise and eulogise the rule of the later medieval counts of Holland. In some instances, this discrepancy was stretched further still, here illustrated using the late thirteenth to early fourteenth-century *Rijmkroniek van Holland*, revised by the comital clerk Melis Stoke:

Doemen screef VIII^c jaer
Ende LXIII over waer,
Karel de Kaluwe zekerlike,
Die coninc was in Vrankerike
Ende van Vrieslant had een deel,
Begonste te stichten al geheel
Hollant uut sinen conincrike.
Want hi gaf enen Dederike
Dese lande, [...]. (Burgers 2004: 12).

(As was written the year eight hundred
and sixty-three, in truth,
Charles the Bald, who was firmly
king of the Frankish realm
and possessed a part of Frisia,
began to fully establish
Holland from his kingdom.
For he gave the one called Dirk
this land [...].)

These details, likewise found in the above-mentioned *Chronographia* (Bruch 1973: 55), present an implausible scenario: not only did Charles the Bald not control these particular lands at any point during his reign, Dirk would have been neither capable nor qualified to take on any viking forces when this supposed transaction took place, having seemingly yet to be born, let alone reach adulthood.[5]

Similar retrofitting may have taken place for Egmond Abbey's own recorded history. Even though the monastic community itself does not predate the tenth century, vikings feature prominently in the first *vita* of its patron, Adalbert, composed around 985. According to the hagiographer, the Northumbrian missionary passed away near Egmond in the early eighth century, whereupon a small chapel was erected over his grave (Vis 1987:

48-51). The shrine is noted to have survived a number of viking incursions due to post-mortem interventions by the saint himself, including the miraculous displacement of a sand dune in the presence of a Scandinavian host (Vis 1987: 56-57). Another regional saint, Jeroen, based at Noordwijk, was purportedly martyred by vikings around 850, upon which his remains were interred and forgotten, only to be rediscovered and translated to Egmond in later centuries (Oppermann 1933: 47-53; Berkum 1993: 60; Mulder-Bakker 2002: 47-48).

As the earliest hagiographies for both saints seem to have been produced beyond any living memory of their respective lives and deaths, their suitability as historical sources may reasonably be called into question. Supported by the counts of Holland, they may have been composed to consciously incentivise local cults of veneration, consolidating Adalbert and Jeroen's position in the abbey's institutional memory. In turn, this association – as well as the local presence of relics – would have expanded Egmond's ecclesiastical centrality as a pilgrimage site. As the perceived antithesis of sanctity, vikings served as a narrative motif to underline the righteousness of these saints and ratify their local worship. Whether factual or fictitious, this continued association between heathens and holy men continued to accentuate the abbey's significance well into the fourteenth and fifteen centuries, as expressed by chronicles produced within and outside its walls, including de Beke's *Chronographia*:

> Hoc eciam tempore sanctus Yeron per dyocesanum episcopum et comitem Theodricum cum miraculis in Egmondam translatus est, qui pridem a Danis in Nortich, [...] martyrii palmam consecutus est. (Bruch 1973: 61).

> (At this time, St. Jeroen, who had previously received the palm of martyrdom from the Danes in Noordwijk, was translated to

Egmond by the diocesan bishop and Count Dirk, surrounded by miracles.)

Over time, other regional authors seem to have composited some of these separate episodes of Scandinavian violence into a single instalment, as seen in the fifteenth-century Middle Dutch chronicle later styled *het Goudse kroniekje*:

> Doe toghen dat wrede heyden volc voert tot noertwijck daer si veel volcs versloeghen ende vinghen. Onder welcke was die heylighe priester sinte ieroen ende wort ghevanghen ende wort onthoeft. Daer na soe toghen si tot egmondt, ende braken daer die heylige kerke die sinte aelbrecht selver hadde ghesticht. (Anonymous 1478: 16r).

> (Then those cruel heathens made their way to Noordwijk, where they killed and captured many people. Among them was the holy priest St. Jeroen, who was captured and beheaded. Afterwards they went to Egmond, and there destroyed the holy church which St. Adalbert himself had founded.)

The versatility with which contemporary chroniclers employed vikings as a narrative device can likewise be seen in late medieval descriptions of Godfrid, a Scandinavian leader who was granted parts of Frisia as a Carolingian benefice in 882 (Waitz 1883: 153; Kurze 1891: 99; Pertz 1829a: 199). Very few details on his tenure exist in contemporary sources, whilst many consecutive authors are silent on the matter altogether. Nevertheless, some historians – including Johannes de Beke (Zeeburgh 1873: 91) – had been able to fill this narrative vacuum by the fourteenth century:

> [...] ac idem Godefridus rex exinde Frisones sibi rebellantes redegit in vile servitutis improperium, ita quod omnes circa collum circumastrictum baiularent laqueum, ut

unumquemque sine mora suspenderet, qui contra maiestatem suam aliquomodo rebellare presumeret. (Bruch 1973: 59).

([...] and the same King Godfrid then reduced the rebelling Frisians to the shame of servitude, such that all of them would carry the burden of a noose around their neck, to be immediately hung by, should they somehow presume to rebel against his majesty.)

In this instance, the Frisians are unequivocally characterised as victims of Scandinavian brutality. Within another century, however, subsequent chroniclers had made subtle yet significant changes to the narrative, as seen in *het Goudse kroniekje*:

Daer nae [...] soe makeden die vriesen een opstal teghen den coninc godeuaert, ende teghens den keyser. Mer doe die coninc kaerl dat vernam, soe quam hi mit soe groter macht in vrieslant, ende bedwancse soe seer [...], soe dat elc vriese moste draghen om den hals een strop van enen bast ghelijc een dief daer mense ter stont aen hanghen mochte of si hem meer staken teghens des keysers moghentheyt. (Anonymous 1478: 17r).

(Afterwards [...] the Frisians rebelled against King Godevaert [Godfrid] and against the emperor. When King Charles [the Fat] heard this, he came with a large host to Frisia, and suppressed them [...], so that every Frisian had to wear a noose around his neck like a thief, to be immediately hung by, should they again oppose the emperor's authority.)

At this point, the Frisians are more explicitly cast as culprit rather than casualty, challenging both Scandinavian *and* Carolingian rule. Although their punishment remains unchanged, Godfrid's role in administering it is completely discounted. Scandinavian influences like these seem to be emphasised and diminished as needed, usually in accordance with prevailing regional political climates at the time of authorship. In this instance, the latter of the two sources may reflect the fifteenth-century animosity of the County of Holland towards the Frisians, who had resisted their political subjugation for many centuries (Huisman 2010: 159-162). As expected, concurrent Frisian chroniclers characterised regional Scandinavian occupation as being a much less acquiescent process. The *Gesta Frisiorum*, for example, recounts – in no uncertain terms – the Frisian opposition against a preceding Godfrid's attempt to subdue the region:

> Recht ghelyc als die weduwe Judith den Hertoghe Olofernes dat hovet afsloech, alsoe is [...] Gotfridus, in syne paulione, oeck wonderlic gheslagen van den Vriesen. [...] hy [meende] die Vriesen weder te bedwinghen ende in den eyghendoem te brenghen [...]. Dem Vriesen ende Sassens worde doe groete blytschap van Gotfridus doet. (Epkema 1853: 298).

> (Like the widow Judith cut off Duke Holofernes' head, so too was Godfrid marvellously killed by the Frisians in his tent. [...] he had meant to subjugate the Frisians and bring them under his rule [...]. The Frisians and Saxons were filled with happiness by Godfrid's death.)

Conclusion

Much like their ninth-century counterparts, the North and its peoples spoke to the imagination of late medieval chroniclers across the Low Countries. Where Carolingian authors often skewed their accounts to depict viking activity as being capricious and indiscriminate, their successors turned this portrayal into an increasingly abstract template of adversarialism. Here was a belligerent and anarchic force of foreign nonbelievers

– a quintessential Other – whose actions could be easily recontextualised to suit a wide range of narrative purposes. As such, incoming vikings, typecast in their anachronistic moulds, remained a familiar ingredient in the codification of various monastic and dynastic foundation myths across the region. These renditions would themselves continue to be transcribed and transformed over the course of numerous generations, subject to patronage and political adherence, until the Scandinavian assailant was as chronologically distant from the late medieval author as that same author is from the present day.

This chapter has provided a preliminary glimpse into the appropriation of the viking phenomenon by late medieval authors across the Low Countries, and represents an initial stride towards a more detailed and comprehensive study of this representation during a formative period of collective politico-cultural memory and identity. In turn, this type of inquiry may serve to benchmark long-term perceptions, trace processes of textual transmission, and compare attitudes towards Viking Age hostility within and beyond this regional landscape of sociopolitical change.

Endnotes

[1] I am indebted to Dr Morgan Boharski for her help with the French translation of this text. All other translations into English by the author, unless stated otherwise.

[2] Whilst primarily associated with Scandinavian endeavour, the term 'viking' is here considered to be occupational rather than ethnic. As such, it is presented as a common noun, with a lowercase initial.

[3] (Near-)contemporary references to viking activity in Liège are found in the *Annales Bertiniani* and Regino's *Chronicon* (Waitz 1883: 153; Kurze 1890: 118).

[4] The development of these institutional histories may likewise be framed against the theoretical conceptions of Benedict Anderson's 'imagined communities' (2006) and Hobsbawm and Ranger's 'invented traditions' (1983), for example.

[5] Rather than Charles the Bald († 877), reference may have been made to his grandson Charles the Simple († 929). A diploma dated 15 June 922, detailing the latter king's conferment of the church of Egmond and its dependencies to Dirk, seems to confirm this notion (Lauer 1949: 286-288).

References

Anonymous (1478). *Die cronike of die hystorie van Hollant van Zeelant ende Vrieslant ende van den Sticht van Utrecht*. Gouda: Gheraert Leeu.

Anderson, B. (2006). *Imagined Communities: Reflections on the Origin and Spread of Nationalism*. 3rd edn. New York: Verso.

Bachrach, B. S. (2001). *Early Carolingian Warfare: Prelude to Empire*. Philadelphia: University of Pennsylvania Press.

Benedictines of St. Vaast (ed.) (1624). *Bibliotheca mundi seu speculi maioris Vincentii Burgundi, praesulis Bellovacensis*. Vol. IV. Douai: Beller.

Berkum, A. H. van (1993). 'De vijf Hollandse kerken van Sint Willibrord', in Vis, G.N.M. (ed.), *Egmond tussen Kerk en wereld*. Hilversum: Verloren, pp. 29-66.

Bormans, S. (ed.) (1877). *Ly Myreur des histors: chronique de Jean des Preis dit d'Outremeuse*. Vol. IV. Brussels: Académie royale de Belgique.

Bormans, S. (ed.) (1880). *Ly Myreur des histors: chronique de Jean des Preis dit d'Outremeuse*. Vol. VI. Brussels: Académie royale de Belgique.

Bruch, H. (ed.) (1973). *Chronographia Johannis de Beke*. The Hague: Nijhoff.

Bruch, H. (1986). 'De eerste graven van Holland', *Holland*, 18, pp. 3-12.

Burgers, J. W. J. (1999). *De Rijmkroniek van Holland en zijn auteurs: Historiografie in Holland door de Anonymus (1280-1282) en de grafelijke klerk Melis Stoke (begin veertiende eeuw)*. Hilversum: Verloren.

Burgers, J. W. J. (ed.) (2004). *Rijmkroniek van Holland (366-1305) door een anonieme auteur en Melis Stoke*. The Hague: Instituut voor Nederlandse Geschiedenis.

Carasso-Kok, M. (1981). *Repertorium van verhalende historische bronnen uit de middeleeuwen*. The Hague: Nijhoff.

Driel, J. van (2012). *Meesters van het woord: Middelnederlandse schrijvers en hun kunst*. Hilversum: Verloren.

Ebels-Hoving, B. (1987). 'Nederlandse geschiedschrijving 1350-1530. Een poging tot karakterisering', in Hoving-Ebels, B. et al. (eds.), *Genoechlicke ende lustige historiën. Laatmiddeleeuwse geschiedschrijving in Nederland*. Hilversum: Verloren, pp. 217-242.

Epkema, E. (ed.) (1853). 'Gesta Frisiorum', in *Die Olde Freesche Cronike*. Leeuwarden: Friesch Genootschap van Geschied-, Oudheid- en Taalkunde, pp. 283-306.

Franz, F. (ed.) (1882). *Die Chronica pontificum Leodiensium: eine verlorene Quellenschrift des 13. Jahrhunderts*. Strasbourg: Karl Trübner.

Heller, J. (ed.) (1880). 'Aegidii Aureaevallensis gesta episcoporum Leodiensium', in *MGH SS XXV*. Hannover: Hahn, pp. 1-129.

Hobsbawm, E. and Ranger, T. (eds.) (1983). *The Invention of Tradition*. Cambridge: Cambridge University Press.

Huisman, J. (2010). 'Beeldvorming en identiteit in het laatmiddeleeuwse Friesland', *It beaken: Tydskrift fan de Fryske Akademy*, 72, pp. 157-174.

Kurze, F. (ed.) (1890). *Reginonis abbatis Prumiensis Chronicon cum continuatione Treverensi*. MGH SRG L. Hannover: Hahn.

Kurze, F. (ed.) (1891). *Annales Fuldenses*. MGH SRG VII. Hannover: Hahn.

Kurze, F. (ed.) (1895). *Annales regni Francorum et annales qui dicuntur Einhardi*. MGH SRG VI. Hannover: Hahn.

Lauer, M. P. (ed.) (1949). *Recueil des actes de Charles III le Simple, roi de France (893-923)*. Paris: Imprimerie Nationale.

Lebecq, S. (2012). 'The New Wiks or Emporia and the Development of a Maritime Economy in the Northern Seas (7th-9th Centuries)', in Gelichi, S. and Hodges, R. (eds.), *From One Sea to Another: Trading Places in the European and Mediterranean Early Middle Ages*. Turnhout: Brepols, pp. 11-21.

Loveluck, C. (2013). *Northwest Europe in the Early Middle Ages, c. AD 600-1150: A Comparative Archaeology*. Cambridge: Cambridge University Press.

Milis, L. J. R. (2006). 'The Carolingian Period (Eighth and Ninth Centuries)', in Blom, J.C.H and Lamberts, E. (eds.), *History of the Low Countries*. 2nd edn. New York: Berghahn, pp. 12-18.

Mol, J. A. and Smithuis, J. (2008). 'De Friezen als uitverkoren volk. Religieus-patriottische geschiedschrijving in vijftiende-eeuws Friesland', *Jaarboek voor middeleeuwse geschiedenis*, 11, pp. 165-204.

Mostert, M. (1993). 'Het klooster en de middeleeuwse samenleving. Egmond en Holland (ca. 900-ca. 1200)', in Vis, G. N. M. (ed.), *Egmond tussen Kerk en wereld*. Hilversum: Verloren, pp. 9-28.

Mulder-Bakker, A. B. (2002). 'Saints without a Past: Sacred Places and Intercessory Power in Saints' Lives from the Low Countries', in Mulder-Bakker, A.B. (ed.), *The Invention of Saintliness*. London: Routledge, pp. 38-57.

Oostrom, F. van (2009). 'The Middle Ages until circa 1400', in Hermans, T. (ed.), *A Literary History of the Low Countries*. Rochester, NY: Camden House, pp. 1-61.

Oppermann, O. (ed.) (1933). *Fontes Egmundenses.* Werken uitgegeven door het Historisch Genootschap, series 3, vol. 61. Utrecht: Kemink.

Pertz, G. H. (ed.) (1829a). 'Annales Vedastini', in *MGH SS II*. Hannover: Hahn, pp. 196-209.

Pertz, G. H. (ed.) (1829b). 'Annales Xantenses', in *MGH SS II*. Hannover: Hahn, pp. 217-236.

Pertz, G. H. (ed.) (1844). 'Chronica Sigeberti Gemblacensis monachi', in *MGH SS VI*. Hannover: Hahn, pp. 300-374.

Pleij, H. (2009). 'The Late Middle Ages and the Age of the Rhetoricians, 1400-1560', in Hermans, T. (ed.), *A Literary History of the Low Countries*. Rochester, NY: Camden House, pp. 63-152.

Prevenier, W. (2000). 'The Low Countries, 1290-1415', in Jones, M. (ed.), *The New Cambridge Medieval History VI: c.1300-c.1415*. Cambridge: Cambridge University Press, pp. 570-594.

Prevenier, W. and Blockmans, W. (1986). *The Burgundian Netherlands*. Cambridge: Cambridge University Press.

Reuter, T. (trans.) (1992). *The Annals of Fulda*. Manchester: Manchester University Press.

Schneidmüller, B. (2002). 'Constructing the Past by Means of the Present: Historiographical Foundations of Medieval Institutions, Dynasties, Peoples, and Communities', in Althoff, G. et al. (eds.), *Medieval Concepts of the Past: Ritual, Memory, Historiography*. Cambridge: Cambridge University Press, pp. 167-192.

Schryver, R. de (1997). *Historiografie: vijfentwintig eeuwen geschiedschrijving van West-Europa*. Leuven: Leuven University Press.

Tilmans, K. (1998). 'Koningen in de Kattendijke-kroniek', in Stuip R.E.V. and Vellekoop, C. (eds.), *Koningen in kronieken*. Hilversum: Verloren, pp. 181-206.

Tilmans, K. (ed.) (2005). *Johan Huyssen van Kattendijke-Kroniek: Die Historie of die Cronicke van Hollant, van Zeelant ende van Vrieslant ende van den Stichte van Utrecht*. The Hague: Instituut voor Nederlandse Geschiedenis.

Utenbroeke, P. and Velthem, L. van (eds.) (1863). *Jacob van Maerlant's Spiegel Historiael*. Vol. III. Leiden: Brill.

Verbij-Schillings, J. (ed.) (1999). *Het Haagse handschrift van heraut Beyeren: Hs. Den Haag, Koninklijke Bibliotheek, 131 G 37*. Hilversum: Verloren.

Vis, G.N.M. (ed.) (1987). 'De Vita sancti Adalberti confessoris' in *Egmond en Berne: twee verhalende historische bronnen uit de middeleeuwen*. Nederlandse historische bronnen VII. The Hague: Nederlands Historisch Genootschap, pp. 1-86.

Waitz, G. (ed.) (1883). *Annales Bertiniani*. MGH SRG V. Hannover: Hahn.

Zeeburgh, J.B. van (1873). *Kritiek der Friesche geschiedschrijving*. The Hague: Nijhoff.

European Trade Networks in the Medieval High North

Miriam Tveit

Introduction

The region of Hálogaland formed a narrow and long strip of land on the western coast of the northern Scandinavian peninsula. The region was successively integrated as a province into the Norwegian Crown between the twelfth and sixteenth centuries. In recent decades, scholars have identified the early fourteenth century as a watershed for this process, as the long fourteenth century saw the implementation of a number of royal reforms (Bjørgo 1982; Bertelsen 2009; Tveit 2013; Hansen 2014). This chapter explores the northern inhabitants' wide-ranging networks of commerce in this period of integration.

Historian Lars Ivar Hansen has substantially broadened our view of the medieval and early modern High North[1] and of the interaction between the northern populations. A point of departure for Hansen (2014: 296) and his multidisciplinary research group (Creating the New North 2017) is to see the history of northern Fennoscandia from a *longue durée* perspective spanning the early Middle Ages to the eighteenth century, which

> [...] has led to new understanding of how the most northerly areas of Europe grew from a situation of open interaction between different ethnic groups to one which saw them become northern peripheries subject to emerging kingdoms with administrative centres further south [...].
> (Holt and Opsahl 2017: 236).

Hansen lines up successive steps (2014: 281-300) and three phases (2005: 363-364) in the development of royal domination of the north: the first phase, in the early part of the high Middle Ages, consists of three aspiring realms, Norway, Sweden and Novgorod, all claiming a right to tax the northern population without counting them as legal subjects.[2] Then, in the second phase, in the last part of the high Middle Ages and in the late Middle Ages, the authorities expanded northwards and developed administrative structures in the region. Finally, in the early modern third phase, these powers claimed territorial rights and domination in the North. These insights are significant for understanding developments in what is often dismissed as a distant and empty corner of pre-modern Europe. However, some aspects of this new narrative require more nuance, such as structures that formed *against* this model of development or were formed *by* it. A linear development from 'open interaction' to subjection by distant southern centres presupposes both a curtailing of interaction in the two later phases and also little support from the northern inhabitants for the state-building project in the first phase. In this model, the 'second phase' of expansion and integration is the vital period of transition. As one essay cannot discuss all these aspects in full, I here examine one particular dimension of the effects of integration of Hálogaland: the nature of the economic networks of the sedentary population in the North and how the period of expansion of royal authority affected them.

The political and economic scene of the High North

At least two ethnic groups coexisted in Hálogaland, the Sámi and the Norse, and according to the author of late twelfth-century *Historia Norvegiæ* 'between them there are frequent trade exchanges going on' (*Historia Norvegiæ*: 78). Both groups were involved in the rich coastal economy and small-scale farming (Bertelsen 2011: 79-84). The official province was bordered in the south by Þrœndalǫg and had a fluid border in the north with Finnmǫrk, meaning 'land of the Sámi' in Old Norse. The political organisation of Hálogaland in the Middle Ages has been discussed at length, with no conclusive consensus (Indrebø 1935; Fladby 1978: 16-21; Bratrein 1984: 34). The institutions of the Norwegian kingdom were gradually introduced in the northern province in the twelfth century, and new structures of organising the province seem to have been imposed by the Norwegian crown in the thirteenth. A general revision of the law and legal system in the 1270s gave Hálogaland equal status in the kingdom to the southern provinces (Tveit 2013: 137). The Church expanded northwards in the wake of the royal administration. In the early 1300s, King Hákon V Magnússon (1299-1319) ensured the favour of the Papacy as the Church expanded beyond the Hálogaland area with the erection of several royal chapels (*DN* I, no. 113). The people of Hálogaland were subjected to the Norwegian Crown and Church in successive steps (Hansen 2014: 282-288).

Finnmǫrk was a vast region with few inhabitants, some nomadic, and a few Norse settlers along the coast (Nielssen 1994: 25). The eastern neighbours, Russian, Karelian and Bjarmian, were almost consistently described in hostile terms in the Norse sources, even though these groups formed nodes in a global trade network and were frequently in contact (Hansen 2011: 355).[3] There was an eastern market for products from marine mammals, like blubber, ropes and hides (Nansen 1911: 409, 431-439; Keller 2010). For centuries, fur and luxury products had been exported from the north, as was most famously described in the account of the tradesman Ohthere, who in the 890s travelled with tusks, hides and fur from Hálogaland to England and the court of King Alfred (*Ohthere's Voyages*). The fur trade was an important income for the Norse chieftains until it was ousted by Russian markets in the thirteenth century (Hansen 2006: 67; Nielssen 2009: 84-85; Hansen and Olsen 2014: 145), but products from marine mammals still played a significant role in trade eastwards. Power struggles between regional magnates in the early Middle Ages spurred on extensive migration from the Scandinavian shores to Iceland (Nielssen 2012: 59-60). Resisting pressure from overlords, several of the northern people, including members of regional elite families, seem to have taken this step too (Nielssen 2012: 66-94). The ties between the settlers on Iceland and the old country were maintained in the next generations, as was knowledge of the trade networks with the Sámi (Keller 2010: 12). In the fourteenth century, Icelandic fish exports also became competitive with those from Hálogaland (Nedkvitne 1983: 60-61; Gardiner and Mehler 2007: 397). The fish trade would from then on dominate the economic scene of the northern Norwegian coast. Dried cod, stockfish, had already arrived at European markets from the twelfth century at the latest, and increased steadily from this period (Nielssen 2014: 194-196). Growing production in the next centuries was due to growing demand on the Continent because of demographic growth and urban development in the twelfth century (Wubs-Mrozewicz 2008: 175-176). The inhabitants of continental Europe needed food for the growing population, particularly in urban centres, and durable food for the many fast days (Nielssen 2014: 194). In return, the Háleygir sought not only grain, but also luxury items and textiles (Bertelsen 2009; Keller 2010: 9).

Controlling the fish trade

The commercial revolution of the thirteenth century, with its professionalisation of mercantile systems across northern Europe, had an impact on the Arctic trade networks (Urbanczyk 1992: 230). Foreign actors in Hálogaland trading directly with the production of stockfish caused the royal fish and the merchants of Bergen to miss out on one of their most important exports. Since the early eleventh century, the Crown imposed a tax on the fisheries, but had few means to secure this income (Bjørgo 1982:

46, n. 7). English, Flemish and German merchant unions already dominated the North Sea trade by the thirteenth century, as well as in Norway (Burkhardt 2007; Nielssen 2014: 289-297). Royal administrators tried to channel all exports through Bergen (Helle 2006: 80-82) and from 1294 forbade foreign merchants from travelling 'ultra Bergas uersus partes boreales' (beyond Bergen to the northern parts) as part of a general policy to control trade (*DN* V, no. 23). Similar regulations were introduced for foreign trade with the Norwegian 'skattlands' (Tributary lands; for this term, see Blomkvist 2011: 167-171), Iceland, Greenland and the Faroes (Imsen 2014: 58). These regulations may have been attempts to control Norwegian exports, which German merchants increasingly dominated, and of which the fish trade was a great part (Helle 2006: 80-86; Burkhardt 2007: 74). In 1313, King Hákon V proclaimed that all legal suits in Hálogaland had to be postponed until after the season (which lasted from February-April), disclosing the interest of the Crown in securing the stockfish industry (*NgL* III, no. 38).

Bergen merchants were now the only ones allowed to travel from the south-west to the North to bring counter-products from the European markets and to collect the fish. This move may have severed the personal bonds between the northern producers and the foreign markets – i.e. the fisheries in the North and the distributors in Germany, Flanders and England. However, the prohibition was strongly reiterated in 1302 (*Ngl* III, no. 15) 1306 (*Ngl* IV: 360) and 1348 (*Ngl* III, no. 83), suggesting that both foreigners and locals ignored it, and that the links between producers and trade partners were rigid.

The fishing station and market in Vágar – in the Lofoten islands – had been the northern coastal centre of the stockfish trade since exports began (Bertelsen 2009). Vágar was also the only place in Hálogaland which might be described as having any urban-like traits (Bjørgo 1982; Bertelsen 2009: 210). Archaeological finds reveal that the town-dwellers were up-to-date on European fashion and trends (Lind 1991a; Brun 1996; Helle 2006: 73), and according to archaeologist Reidar Bertelsen, the continuity in the findings from 1200-1400 reveals close contacts with western European networks, due to the town's central position for fish export (2009: 203). There might have been a growing number of foreign merchants coming to Vágar themselves to participate in the stockfish fair in June, or to deal with the producers directly.

Trade networks and social fabrics

What was the essence of the network that developed from the fisheries? The fish trade was arguably more egalitarian than the fur trade, since fisheries on the coast of Hálogaland involved many local farmers who were also fishermen (Nielssen 2009: 84). However, there was a growing class of magnates being enriched by the fisheries. The wealth of the political and economic elite in Vágar and Hálogaland was duly demonstrated in 1335, as a listed dowry specified 74 items for a wedding in Vágar (*DN* IV, no. 217; Elstad 1976). The bride, Jngibiarghar, was the daughter of Jwar the lawman, a regional high official. The groom, Þorlæifr, was the son of Sigurðr with the byname *bonde*, indicating that they were estate-holders with *oðal* (allodial land, see Robberstad et al. 1967). The dowry consisted of items representing the full extent of the northern networks, with an English wool carpet, four high quality items of German cloth and a coffer with 'iarnað a þyðesko' (German ironwork) (*DN* IV, no. 217: 191), as well as fine fur from miniver, vair of sable and grey and red squirrels, probably acquired through the eastern trade networks or from inland Sámi manufacturers. A couple of cloths were also labelled as 'norrœn' (Norse), suggesting the clothes were considered to be made by Norse artisans, probably as a contrast to the display of outlandish property (*DN* IV, no. 217: 191). It is not possible from this list to establish any direct contacts with foreign traders, but neither is it essential. The rich dowry reveals that the wedding was between the elite in Hálogaland society, and, even if every foreign item was procured through mediators or at the market in Vágar, the couple could count themselves among the European elite (Bertelsen 1991: 59; Lind 1991b: 140).

The fourteenth century saw more changes to the distribution networks of the fish trade. In a Prescription from 1384, the Dano-Norwegian royal administration stated that towns and markets, among them Vágar, were 'damaged and deserted, because merchants no longer came with their goods to the traditional market towns' (*NgL* III, no. 104). What had happened to the fishermen's contact points? Already in 1299, King Hákon V demanded that traders hold their business in towns and designated markets (*NgL* III, no. 12), something that was repeated in 1372 (*NgL* III, no. 101). The prescription demanded that merchants from Bergen sail to the market in Vágar, suggesting they at some point had stopped coming north. This is traditionally explained by the impact of the plague (Falkanger 2007: 64), an explanation that has been downplayed in later years (Moseng 2006; Røskaft 2015: 368-373). Nevertheless, instead of the Bergen merchants sailing north, a new system developed in which transport was organised from the northern communities themselves, which involved equipping a *jekt*, a cargo vessel, and sailing to Bergen with the products (Kiil 1993: 18-29), in what Hansa merchants called *Nordfahrer* (Nedkvitne 1983: 292-293). This system would remain in place for five centuries. However, the crown retained its interest in confining trade to the places where it could obtain revenue, and collective repackaging and redistribution in Vágar was due before departure to Bergen. The prescription of 1384 therefore specifically targeted transactions taking place in the fjords and on the fishing stations, called *fiorda koup* and *verija koup*, as illegal (*NgL* III, no. 104). This means transactions were taking place directly between some traders and producers, both ignoring taxes. Evidently, foreign merchants lurked in the seawaters of Hálogaland whilst local producers profited by trading directly with them. Moreover, a contemporary case involving parties from Hálogaland accused of illegal trade with Greenland and Iceland suggests the Háleygir did not always bother to go via Bergen themselves or acquire the necessary permissions (*DN* XVIII, no. 33). Although the parties involved in this illegal trade were pardoned – since they swore to have acted in desperation (their ship needed tending) – it is evident that the northerners had the knowledge, networks and means to conduct exports themselves. The attempts to control trade in the fourteenth century only demonstrate the resilience of the connections between the northern inhabitants and the market.

Another strong connection was the relationship the northern population enjoyed within the fish trade network. Each *Nordfahrer* often nursed a relationship with one particular buyer in the harbour of Bergen, and due to the bartered goods that the northerners brought home, most held big credit with their Bergen merchant (Nielsen 2009: 85-86). Until recently, this relationship has been interpreted as a disadvantage to the *Nordfahrer* and the fisher-farmer family in the north. These days, however, the credit is interpreted as a mutual exploitation, forging a strong relationship between seller and buyer in which the seller gained access to necessary equipment and supplies, and also luxury items, and the buyer had a steady supply of products (Burkhardt 2007; Wubs-Mrozewicz 2008: 149-150). As Arnved Nedkvitne (1983: 372-376) has shown, the *Nordfahrer* might have benefited from this system. The financing of costly northern German and Flemish church art for the chapels in Hálogaland in the fifteenth century tells us that at least some of the suppliers or boat owners (*skipper*) became wealthy (Bergesen 2015: 233-234; Røskaft 2015: 391). The wealth also attracted southern aristocrats to invest in property in the north, such as the knight Tidke Vistenakr, who in 1411 tried to reclaim the goods and fishing grounds he had lost in a case by the lawman in Hálogaland (*DN* II, no. 580, no. 587; *DN* III, no. 603). At this point, the lawman evidently had obtained full jurisdiction for matters in the region that had become a fully-fledged part of the royal legal system. The legal integration of Hálogaland, one could argue, gave economic autonomy to the region.

The narratives of Italian merchants who shipwrecked on their way to Flanders in 1432 and landed on the skerries outside the Lofoten archipelago give insight into the effects of trade in normal fishing communities in Hálogaland (De Cardini 1480 [1431]; Ramvsio 1983 [1606]). Venetian Captain Pietro Querini, shipmate Cristophoro Fioravante and the rest of the surviving crew spent the winter in the care of fisher-families at the island of Røst before returning home. In what he thought to be an outpost of Europe, Querini found the common inhabitants to be wealthy, dressed in rich (grossa) woollen cloth 'from London and other places' (Ramvsio 1983 [1606]: 204r), while Fioravante remarks that although they have plenty of their currency, the stockfish, they mainly dressed in leather or inexpensive, coloured cloth from Denmark (Ramvsio 1983 [1606]: 209v). Both depictions speak of European influences through the fish trade.

The prosperous trade had ripple effects in the region that were not exclusive to population identified with the Norse. From early on in the stockfish trade, Sámi groups were both involved in the fisheries and supplied the industry with vital equipment, including boats (Hansen 2006: 66-67; Nielssen 2009: 84; Nielssen 2014: 287-289). Sámi living inland were also connected to the fish trade through bartering (Hansen 2011: 355). The understanding of a relationship moving from open interaction to a subordination of minority groups is partly based on descriptions of a reciprocal tax-trade relationship with the Sámi according to Hansen's first phase, as described by Ohthere (*Ohthere's Voyages*: 250-251), changing to taxation that involved extracting tribute from the Sámi in the third phase (Hansen 2014: 296). A commercial reciprocal dependence between the groups still materialised in the middle period.

Traders and raiders

There had also been great changes in the Scandinavian political scene of the fourteenth century; a Swedish-Norwegian union was formed in 1319, and in 1397, the three Scandinavian kingdoms and their overseas 'skattlands' entered into the Kalmar Union. Scandinavian rulers could now concentrate their efforts on the northern region. From 1319, the Kalmar Union was headed by young King Magnus IV/VII Eiríksson (1319-1374); in Norway, the country was governed under the regency of a state council headed by the protector Erlingr Viðkunsson, from what is considered the most powerful kin-group in Hálogaland through the Middle Ages, the Bjarkey kin-group (Eidnes 1956). During this reign, three treaties cut out a common area in the High North between Russian, Swedish and Norwegian authorities. These were the peace treaty between Sweden and Novgorod from 1323 (*Peace treaty of Nöteborg*), the peace treaty between Norway and Novgorod of 1326 (*NgL* III, no. 65a) and a border treaty with a suggested date of 1330 (*NgL* III, no. 65b). The treaties defined the borders between the realms, but these realms also acknowledged a double set of borders in the north, which Carsten Pape has interpreted as comprising an outer and inner border line (Pape 2004: 178-180). The intermediate space comprised a large common area between the realms. In overlapping regions, this arrangement meant that two or all three kingdoms could extract revenue and tax (Gallén 1991; Lind 2000; Hansen 2005: 368-374). A notable aspect of these treaties, also noted by Hansen (2011: 356-357), is their concern with protecting the rights of traders. The Russian treaty with the Swedish king (in 1323) stated that *Mercatores* from 'Almania, Lubech, Gotlandia et Suechie terra' without impediment could traverse the common territory, while the treaty with the Norwegian king, three years later, stressed the same rights for the *hospites* (visitors, strangers), obviously referring to the merchants and nomads roaming the area and traveling between the Norwegian and Russian sides (*NgL* III, no. 65a: 152). The treaty otherwise urged forgiving prior instances of trespassing and harm, which is notable given that the Bjarkey-estate of protector Erlingr Viðkunsson was destroyed in a raid by Karelian marauders three years earlier (*Icelandic Annals*: 346), the same year of the first peace treaty in the name of King Magnus IV/VII. Erlingr, as head of the council, must have been involved in the later treaty. The Bjarkey kin-group of Erlingr was deeply involved in the trade over Fennoscandia, as well as the continental fish trade, but favoured peaceful collaboration over personal vengeance. The bilateral interests in these treaties were obviously to secure income from the lucrative northern trade networks, but also to stimulate trade between ethnic groups.

Correspondence between the Kalmar King Eric of Pomerania (1381/82-1459) and King Henry VI of England (1421-1471) reveals that German and English merchants still traded along the northern coasts in the 1420s and 1430s (*DN* I, no. 670; *DN* XX no. 776, 779, 796). This could be an effect of ongoing rivalry between Dutch and English merchants with the Hanseatic League (Burkhardt 2007: 71-78). Nevertheless, unofficial European trade networks still survived in this part of the Kalmar Union.

Conclusion

Did the subjection by distant southern centres in Hansen's 'second phase' curtail the networks of the northern population? Although this small study on the nature of the trade networks is by no means conclusive, it has revealed that networks to the east and west both thrived and were encouraged by royal politics in the long fourteenth century. Royal authorities increasingly regulated trade in the north, whilst nevertheless arranging for open interaction between the region's ethnic groups. The northern inhabitants' trade networks were stimulated, not dictated, by this development, counter to the overall development of subordination. The northern region became closer to the southern-centred economy and politics, but the inhabitants were integral members of a variety of international networks after this process of integration. When the administrative infrastructure was established in the northern provinces of the Norwegian kingdom, actors simultaneously became more autonomous at using these new administrative tools. The northern population gained the means to exploit fully economic networks, even if the contacts were – to a large degree – defined, instigated and controlled by the politics of the Crown.

Endnotes

[1] 'High North' in this context is a phrasing used as a nuanced alternative to 'Far North'. The term 'High North' is more accurate, and avoids the connotations of being far removed from an Anglo-Continental centre.

[2] The time frames are set in accordance with the Norwegian Middle Ages, where the traditional form of division is early Middle Ages c. 750-1030, high Middle Ages 1030-c. 1350 and late Middle Ages c. 1350-1537.

[3] The etymology behind the term 'Biarmian' is widely discussed, as is defining the ethnic identity and homeland of the Bjarmian people. Ohthere (*Ohthere's Voyages*: 248) described the 'Biarmian' area to the south coast of White Sea, and the northern parts of the Dvina river valley. They are today identified with the Baltic-Finnish speaking peoples, known as the Vepsians or the Chudes. See Hansen and Olsen (2014: 149-150).

References

Bergesen, R. H. (2015). 'Billedprogrammet på Trondenes: Den hellige Anna–sjømennenes og rikdommens beskytter'. *Nordlit*, 15, 229-248.

Bertelsen, R. (1991). 'Periferi og periferidannelse fra førhistorisk til historisk tid'. *Gunneria*, 64, pp. 51-71.

Bertelsen, R. (2009). 'Vágar, en kortlevd by eller et urbant fiskevær?', in Brendalsmo, J., Eliassen, F. E. and Gansum, T. (ed.), *Den urbane underskog, Strandsteder, utvekslingssteder og småbyer i vikingtid, middelalder og tidlig nytid*, Oslo: Interface Media, pp. 199-211.

Bertelsen, R. (2011). 'Tilkomsten av fiskevær, med særlig blikk på kysten mellom Vestfjorden og Lopphavet', in Hansen, L. I, Holt, R. and Steinar I. (eds.), *Nordens plass i middelalderens nye Europa, Samfunnsomdannin, sentralmakt og periferier*, Stamsund: Orkana Akademisk, pp. 78-88.

Bjørgo, N. (1982). 'Vågastemna i mellomalderen', in Imsen, S. and Sandvik, G. (eds.), *Hamarspor, Eit festskrift til Lars Hamre 1912-1982*, Oslo: Universitetsforlaget, pp. 45-60.

Blomkvist, N. (2011). 'The skattland – a Concepts Suitable for Export? The Role of Loosely Integrated Territories in the Emergence of the Medieval State', in Imsen, S. (ed.), *Taxes, Tributes and Tributary Lands in the Making of the Scandinavian Kingdoms in the Middle Ages*, Trondheim: Tapir Academic Press, pp. 167-188.

Bratrein, H. D. (1984). 'Skjøttebåter og leidangsskip i Nord-Norge'. *Acta Borealia*, 1(1), 27-37.

Brun, T. A. (1996). 'Mellomalderkeramikk. Et perifert materiale i det sentrale Nord-Norge'. Master Thesis. University of Tromsø.

Burkhardt, M. (2007). 'One Hundred Years of Thriving Commerce at a Major English Sea Port—The Hanseatic Trade at Boston between 1370 and 1470', in Brand, H., Holm, P. and L. Müller (eds.), *The Dynamics of Economic Culture in the North Sea and Baltic Region (c. 1250-1700)*, Vol 1, Hilversum: Verloren, pp. 65-85.

Creating the New North (2017), 'English summary'. Available at: https://en.uit.no/forskning/forskningsgrupper/gruppe?p_document_id=344565 (Accessed: 01 March 2018).

De Cardini, A. D. C. ([1431] 1480). *Relazione del naufragio della 'Coca Quirina', Venezia, 8 ottobre 1480, sul racconto di Cristofalo Fioravante e Nicolò de Michiele*, Biblioteca Nazionale Marciana Venezia, BNMVe, It. VII, 368 (=7936).

DN = *Diplomatarium Norvegicum*, in *Diplomatarium Norvegicum, Oldbreve til Kundskab om Norges indre og ydre Forhold, Sprog, Slægter, Sæder, Lovgivning og Rettergang i Middelalderen*, (1847-1990). Vol 1-22, 1849-1990. Christiania/Oslo: varia.

Eidnes, H. (1956). 'Bjarkøy og Bjarkøyætta', *Håløygminne*, 9, 560-565.

Elstad, K. (1976). 'Eit storbryllaup i Vågan på 1300-tallet', in *Skolp, Årbok for Vågan*, 1, pp. 11-16.

Falkanger, A. T. (2007). *Lagmann og lagting i Hålogaland: gjennom 1000 år*. Oslo: Universitetsforlaget.

Fladby, R. (1978). *Hvordan Nord-Norge ble styrt-Nordnorsk administrasjonshistorie fra 1530-åra til 1660*, Oslo: Universitetsforlaget.

Gallén, J. (1991). *Nöteborgsfreden och Finlands medeltida östgräns*, Vol. 2, Helsinki: Svenska Litteratursällskapet i Finland.

Gardiner, M., and Mehler, N. (2007). 'English and Hanseatic Trading and Fishing Sites in Medieval Iceland: Report on Initial Fieldwork'. *Germania*, 85 (2), 385-427.

Hansen, L. I. (2005). 'Fra Nöteborgsfreden til Lappekodisillen, ca. 1300-1751. Folkegrupper og statsdannelse på Nordkalotten med utgangspunkt i Finnmark', in Imsen, S. (ed.), *Grenser og grannelag i Nordens historie*. Oslo: Cappelen Damm Akademisk, pp. 362-386.

Hansen, L. I. (2006). 'Sami Fisheries in the Pre-Modern Era. Household Sustenance and Market Relations', *Acta Borealia*, 23 (1), pp. 56-80.

Hansen, L. I. (2011). 'The Russian-Norwegian Border in Medieval and Early Modern Times', in Olsen, B., Urbanczyk, P.

and Amundsen, C. (eds.). *Hybrid Spaces: Medieval Finnmark and the Archaeology of Multi-room Houses*. Oslo: Novus Press, pp. 355-67.

Hansen, L. I. (2014). 'Successive Integration of Hålogaland and Finnmork into the Realm of the King of Norway', in Imsen, S. (ed.), *Rex Insularum: The King of Norway and His "Skattlands" as a Political System c. 1260-c. 1450*. Bergen: Fagbokforlaget, pp. 347-369.

Hansen, L. I. and Olsen, B. (2014). *Hunters in Transition. An Outline of Early Sami History*. Leiden: Brill.

Helle, K. (2006). *Norsk byhistorie: urbanisering gjennom 1300 år*. Oslo: Pax.

Historia Norvegiæ = Storm, G. (ed.) (1973). *Monumenta historica Norvegiæ: latinske kildeskrifter til Norges historie i middelalderen*. Kristiania: Norsk historisk kjeldeskrift-institutt, pp. 69-124.

Holt, R. and Opsahl, E. (2017). 'Boundaries and Borders', in Berg, S. H., Tveit, M. and Vogt, H. (eds.) *'It's all about inheritance' – On Gender, Sámi, Bourdieu and other Important Categories in Lars Ivar Hansen's Research, Speculum Boreale*, Tromsø: Universitetet i Tromsø, pp. 235-239.

Icelandic Annals = Storm, G. (ed.) (1888). *Islandske Annaler indtil 1578*. Kristiania: Det norske historiske kildeskriftfond.

Imsen, S. (2014). 'Royal Dominion in the "Skattlands"', in Imsen, S. (ed.) *Rex Insularum: The King of Norway and His "Skattlands" as a Political System c. 1260-c. 1450*. Bergen: Fagbokforlaget, pp. 35-99.

Indrebø, G. (1935). *Fjordung: granskingar i eldre norsk organisasjons-soge*. Bergen: Bergens Museums Årbok.

Keller, C. (2010). 'Furs, Fish, and Ivory: Medieval Norsemen at the Arctic Fringe'. *Journal of the North Atlantic*, 3 (1), pp. 1-23.

Kiil, A. (1993). *Da bøndene seilte: bygdefarsbrukets historie i Nordlandene*. Oslo: Messel.

Lind, J. (2000). 'The Russian-Swedish Border according to the Peace Treaty of Nöteborg (Orekhovets-Pähkinälinna) and the Political Status of the Northern Part of Fennoscandia'. *Mediaeval Scandinavia*, 13, pp. 100-117.

Lind, K. E. (1991a). 'Sko som materiell kultur, Vågarsamfunnet i middelalderen'. Magister thesis. University of Tromsø.

Lind, K. E. (1991b). 'Arkeologisk innsikt i Vågans rolle fra høymiddelalder til seinmiddelalder'. *Gunneria*, 64, pp. 135-45.

Moseng, O. G. (2006). *Den flyktige pesten: vilkårene for epidemier i Norge i seinmiddelalder og tidlig nytid.* Unpublished Doctoral Thesis. Universitetet i Oslo.

Nansen, F. (1911). *Nord i tåkeheimen: utforskningen av jordens nordlige strøk i tidlige tider.* Kristiania: Dybwad.

Nedkvitne, A. (1983). *Utenrikshandelen fra det vestafjelske Norge 1100-1600.* Unpublished Doctoral Thesis. Universitetet i Bergen.

NgL = Norges gamle Love I-III (1846-49), Keyser, R., Munch, P. A., and Storm, G. (eds.). Kristiania: Grøndahl.

Nielssen, A. R. (1994). 'The Importance of the Hanseatic Trade for the Norwegian Settlement in Finnmark', in Henn, V. and Nedkvitne. A. (eds.), *Norwegen und die Hanse: Wirtschaftliche und kulturelle Aspekte im europäischen Vergleich*, Frankfurt a.M.: Peter Lang, pp. 19-30.

Nielssen, A. R. (2009). 'Norwegian Fisheries, c. 1100–1850', in Starkey, D. J. and Heidbrink, I. (eds.), *A History of the North Atlantic Fisheries.* Bremen: Hauschild, pp. 83-122.

Nielssen, A. R. (2012). *Landnåm fra nord: utvandringa fra det nordlige Norge til Island i Vikingtid.* Stamsund: Orkana Akademisk.

Nielssen, A. R. (2014). 'Markedsretting og nasjonal betydning av fiskeriene 1000-1350', in Kolle, N. et al. (eds.), *Norges fiskeri- og kysthistorie. Bind I: Fangstmenn, fiskerbønder og værfolk. Fram til 1720.* Bergen: Fagbokforlaget, pp. 187-299.

Ohthere's Voyages = Thorpe, B. (transl.) (1902). *The Life of Alfred the Great: Translated from the German of Dr R. Pauli; to which is Appended Alfred's Anglo-Saxon Version of Orosius.* London: George Bell and Sons, pp. 248-253.

Pape, C. (2004). 'Rethinking the Medieval Russian-Norwegian border', *Jahrbücher für Geschichte Osteuropas*, (H. 2), 161-187.

Peace treaty of Nöteborg = *Diplomatarium Fennicum*, no. 313. In *Finlands medeltidsurkunder. Samlade och i tryck utgifna af Finlands Statsarkiv genom Reinh. Hausen* (1910), Vol I. Helsinki: Finlands Statsarkiv, pp. 121-125.

Ramvsio, G. B. (1983 [1606]). 'Viaggio del Magnifico Messer Piero Qvirino Gentil hvomo Vititiano' and 'Navfragio del Sopradetto Messer Piero Qvirino Descritto', in *Delle navigationi et viaggi*, 2, ff. 199v-211r.

Robberstad, K. et al. (1967). 'Odelsrett', in *Kulturhistorisk Leksikon for Nordisk Middelalder*, vol. 12. Copenhagen: Rosenkilde og Bagger, pp. 493-503.

Røskaft, M. (2015), 'Håløygriket blir en landsdel', in Holberg, E. and Røskaft, M., *Håløygriket, Nordlands historie 1, Før 1600*. Bergen: Fagbokforlaget, pp. 219-436.

Tveit, M. (2013). 'The Introduction of a Law of the Realm in Northern Norway', in Imsen, S. (ed.), *Legislation and State Formation, Norway and its Neighbours in the Middle Ages*, Trondheim: Akademika, pp. 41-54.

Urbanczyk, P. (1992). *Medieval Arctic Norway*. Warsaw: Semper.

Wubs-Mrozewicz, J. (2008). *Traders, Ties and Tensions: The Interactions of Lübeckers, Overijsslers and Hollanders in Late Medieval Bergen*. Hilversum: Verloren.

Runes in Orkney: Making a Diaspora a Home?

Andrea Freund

Norse Orkney is marked by an abundance of runic inscriptions in a relatively small archipelago. Fifty-five Viking Age or medieval runic inscriptions are counted within its corpus (*Samnordisk Runtextdatabas* 2018).[1] This chapter examines in detail how runic writing has contributed to the formation of identity in Orkney as part of the Norse diaspora. It considers questions such as: were runes deliberately used to mark Orkney as a Norse home? Can runic writing in Orkney be regarded as part of a claim for Norse overlordship of the land or did it form part of everyday activities the Norse took to Orkney from their homelands? By taking an interdisciplinary approach to the Orcadian corpus of runic inscriptions, using research from linguistics, archaeology and toponymy with a theoretical background in diaspora studies and Bakhtin's model of heteroglossia, this chapter examines aspects of the corpus. Connections across the sea, questions of status and linguistic change are considered to evaluate if, and to what extent, runes were used in Orkney to claim it as home and how this reflects identity formation.

The earliest Norse settlement in Orkney dates probably to the mid-ninth century (Barrett and Richards 2004). Before this period, Orkney was culturally part of Pictland, likely under the overlordship of Pictish kings (Lamb 1993). The extent of the first Norse settlement, the fate of the Pictish population, and the mechanisms by which the Norse gained control are still debated (Sanmark 2017: 194-196). With the establishment of the Norse earldom in c. 875, Orkney formally fell under the Norwegian crown and remained so until 1468. It became a Norwegian 'skattland' (tributary land),[2] with a fully Norse legal system and strong economic ties to Norway (Thomson 2008). The only contemporary sources written in Orkney from the first Norse settlement until the late thirteenth century are runic inscriptions.

Before discussing Orkney as part of the Norse diaspora, it is helpful to define what exactly diaspora means in this context and how it relates to the Norse in Orkney. Jesch explains diaspora as 'an ongoing connectedness that came out of a migrational event or events' (2015: 81). Within a diaspora, hybrid identities can develop through the influence of different factors than in the homeland (Curtin 1984; Kalra, Kalhon and Hutynuk 2005: 30). Hence, being part of a diaspora itself has an influence on identity negotiations. When runic inscriptions in the diaspora are viewed as expressions of identity, it should be expected that they differ from the homeland if this argument holds for Orkney. In a recent study, Barrett concludes that, while the Scandinavian diaspora as such is a wide-spread phenomenon, there is a diversity of extremely local expressions of distinctive, sometimes hybrid identities (Barrett 2015: 2-5). In the context of this chapter, an important question is whether the development of distinctive local identities is mirrored in the runic evidence, which would support Barrett's argument.

The currently known Scandinavian runic inscriptions from Orkney can be split into thirty-three from inside the Neolithic chambered tomb of Maeshowe (detailed in Barnes 1994) and twenty-two from the rest of Orkney (inscriptions found before 2006 listed in Barnes and Page 2006, further new finds in Barnes 2015 and Ljosland forthcoming, see Appendix for list). Two inscriptions which used to be counted in the corpus, OR 2 and OR 13, are now known to be modern (Barnes and Page 2006: 338-340; Freund and Ljosland 2019). OR 5, on a small stone, is lost and only recorded in one photograph from 1908 and might have been a modern carving copying a rune of OR 4 or from Maeshowe

(Barnes and Page 2006: 165-166). OR 7's medieval origins are at least doubtful, too (Barnes and Page 2006: 172-174). Of the twenty remaining Viking Age and medieval inscriptions from outside Maeshowe, four are from islands other than the Orcadian mainland (Westray, Rousay, Sanday and Burray).

The materials used are very diverse. Only seven (of which three, OR 8, OR 9 and OR 16, could have been the same inscription) are most likely fragments of runestones with the classic memorial inscription 'X raised this stone in memory of Y'.[3] The largest number of inscriptions which can be dated with some certainty come from the early to mid-twelfth century, which means most of the corpus post-dates the Viking Age.

Some of the Orcadian runic inscriptions show variations in their language, wording or style which can be used to trace connections to both the Scandinavian mainland and the diaspora. Some inscriptions which contain idiomatic expressions point to either Norway or the West Norse diaspora, such as Iceland (e.g. the Icelandic idiom 'fyrir sunnan land' [in the south of the country], i.e. Iceland, in OR Barnes 20). The rune forms, phonology and orthography of inscriptions, particularly inside Maeshowe, show the largest resemblance with Norwegian examples, and where a dialectal variety of Old Norse can be ascertained, it is West Norse (Barnes 1994: 48-60).

As for the style and type of inscribed objects, there are both connections to Norway, as in memorial stones (compare the layout of OR 17, with the inscription on the narrow side of the slab, with that of the Kuli stone, N 449); Denmark, where folded lead plates as amulets are most commonly found and probably originate from (Steenholt Olesen 2010); and Greenland where the fashion for inscribed textile tools, such as spindle whorls, appears to begin (Imer 2017: 73-79). Another Greenlandic connection in the Orcadian corpus is shown by the use of the 'Greenlandic' variety of the r-rune in OR 10. This variety occurs twenty-one times in Greenland, twice in Iceland on portable objects and at least four times in Norway (Imer 2017: 42). The carver of OR 10 need not necessarily have been a Greenlander but it seems likely they had previously encountered the variety.

It is not only rune forms and spellings in Orkney that show connections across the sea; in two instances inscribed objects themselves have travelled from Scandinavia or within the diaspora. OR 11 is inscribed with the first six runes of the Younger Futhark. Its recent identification as a bear's tooth means the object, with or without runes, must have been imported as it is assumed from archaeological records that brown bears became extinct in the British Isles, including Orkney, during the Roman period (Hull 2007; Yalden 1999). The origin of the tooth may be mainland Scandinavia, but without isotope analysis it is impossible to ascertain. Seeing as it is one of the earlier objects in the Orcadian corpus and comes from one of the earliest Norse settlements on the Orcadian Mainland, it is possible that a settler could have brought it with them.

Another inscribed portable object, OR 3, a spindle whorl, was discovered in Stromness but its material, steatite, makes it likely that this object was also imported at some point in its production process because steatite has never been quarried in Orkney (Sindbæk 2015). It is impossible to tell when the object was brought to Orkney and where the runes were carved.

When considered together, all these aspects show that Orkney was well-connected with both the homeland and other Norse settlements so that innovations and fashions in runic writing were quickly adopted and relayed onwards. The processes evident in runic writing and the objects being inscribed fit the model Hall (1990) postulates for cultural identities: external circumstances and connections influence the formation and expression of diaspora identities in Orkney but there remains a strong connection to the culture of the homeland.

An important part of identity formation and discussion of identity in past societies is social status (Babić 2005: 67). In this regard, some information can be drawn from analysing the status of the sites where runic inscriptions are found in Orkney. In case of runestone fragments, it is justifiable to assume that they would have been carved somewhere near their findspot even if the fragments have been re-used in later buildings. Hence, the place-names and archaeology of their findspot can be examined to determine if the inscription has likely been carved at a high-status site.

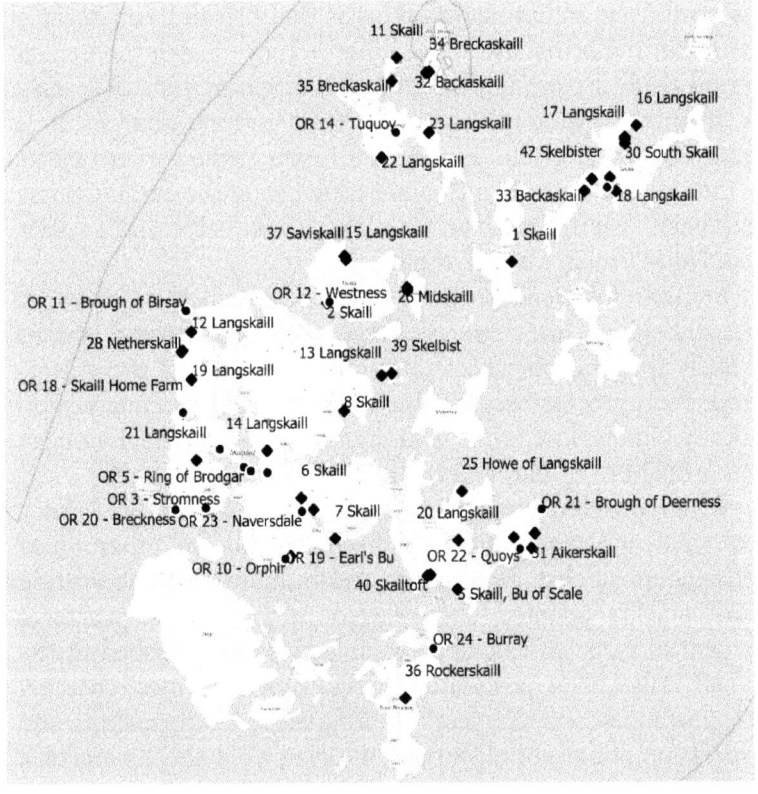

Fig. 1: *Map of runic findspots in Orkney in relation to Skaill/*skaill place-names. Made by the author with data from Thomson (2012).*

When mapped out (Fig. 1), most findspots of immovable objects appear reasonably close to at least one high-status Norse site, be it marked out through archaeology, such as the Brough of Birsay for OR 6, OR 8, OR 9, OR 11 and OR 16 (Morris 1989) and Earl's Bu in Orphir for OR 10, OR 15 and OR 19 (Batey and Morris 1989), or toponymy, most prominently the Skaill/*skaill (from ON *skáli* – shed/hut) names across the archipelago which indicate the site of a hall (Thomson 2012). Only two current place-names of findspots can be interpreted at indicating low-status sites, namely Tuquoy and Quoys. Both names are derived from ON *kví*, 'cattle-fold', denoting an enclosure. This toponym appears usually relatively late in Orkney, not for primary Norse settlements (Marwick 1952: 227-229). Seeing as OR 14 dates from the Viking Age to early medieval phase of the site at Tuqouy (Barnes and Page 2006: 200), it could reasonably pre-date the formation of the place-name. OR 22 is a stray find and a small, portable object (Barnes 2015: 144-146), so it does not necessarily have to be associated with the place-name Quoys at all. In general, the toponymy of findspots in Orkney leans more towards high-status place-names than should be expected from an average distribution. This implies that runic writing was practised more frequently at high-status sites in the archipelago, so there is a connection between high social status and expressing one's identity in the Norse writing system of the homeland.

Another important aspect of identity, especially in a diaspora setting where linguistic change occurs, such as the transformation from a predominantly Celtic-speaking population to the exclusive use of Old Norse in Orkney, is linguistic identity.[4] Bakhtin's model of centrifugal and centripetal forces on language and linguistic change explains that the further a speaker is removed from centres of power and authority over language, the greater the variety and changes of their speech. Bakhtin argues that due to the nature of language as dialogic and discursive it is constantly subject to unifying, centripetal forces and digressing, centrifugal forces, leading to heteroglossia. These forces are caused by both ideology and individuality, and any utterance contributes to further heteroglossia through dialogue (Bakhtin 2006: 271-275). This model is normally applied to spoken language as in Bakhtin's original work and not to runic inscriptions but, as it is usually assumed that runic spelling follows pronunciation and inscriptions reflect spoken language relatively closely (Williams 1990: 10-14; though see Barnes and Page 2006: 73 for criticism), it may be assumed that the carvings are close enough to the speech act for this model to be useful. Particularly in Orkney with its low number of inscriptions using the standardised memorial formula the corpus should reflect developments in the spoken language enough for Bakhtin's model to be applicable. In a diaspora context, it is therefore expected that, with increasing distance from the homeland, the language should change at a more rapid pace if central authority being exerted by the homeland becomes weaker, and in the case of Orkney, this should also be reflected in the runic inscriptions. However, in contrast to Caithness, where SC 11 – Thurso I contains the neologism 'ubirlak' (overlay) (Barnes and Page 2006: 237-243), no such linguistic variation can be found in the Orcadian corpus despite it being much larger than the corpus of runic inscriptions from mainland Scotland. Potentially, centrifugal forces in Orkney, the closest Norwegian 'skattland' to the mainland, were not as dominant as in other Norse colonies, but equally this could constitute a conscious alignment of the social stratum using runes with Norwegian authority.

In the entire corpus, twenty-eight personal names are identifiable beyond doubt with two more probable cases. The largest number is Norse in origin, with the Biblical names Benedikt, Simon (OR Barnes 22/29) and Philippus (OR 6) as the only exceptions. There is not a single Gaelic, or Norse version of a Gaelic, personal name in the corpus. One could now assume that this means a predominantly Norse cultural affiliation. However, these names might have been used because they belong to the

Norse sphere of a multi-layered identity. The idea of a person using two different names at the same time but for different purposes was not unknown in medieval Northern Europe. A prime example is *Gunhildskorset* (Gunhildr's Cross; *Samnordisk Runtextdatabas*: DR 413), a cross from walrus ivory inscribed with a prayer in Latin which has both runes and Roman letters. It is dated to c. AD 1100. In line D, the inscription says in normalised Latin in Roman letters: '[...] Helene que et Gunhild vocatur' (Helene who is also called Gunhildr), while Gunhildr also appears a second time, this time in runes. This means that one woman could have a Norse and a Latin name. It is interesting that Gunhildr appears in runes but not Helena. This could indicate a preference of using a Norse name for runes while a name of Latin or Greek origin was not considered suitable to be carved in runes in this case. There is no indication of the underlying reasons, but it proves that the idea of a Norse name and a second name from another language is plausible and similar arrangements for Orkney are thinkable. In addition, if this idea is taken to its logical conclusion, the idea of Norse names being more suitable for carving runes would imply that the number of Norse names in the Orcadian corpus, particularly Maeshowe, cannot be used to claim a purely Norse origin or cultural identity of these named individuals. It might equally indicate a simple preference for using the Norse name of a person known under various names when using runes, with the three exceptions mentioned above, similar to the contemporaneous practice in Denmark.

An accepted feature of modern bilingual societies is that people often use two names, one in each language, and exclusively employ the names depending on the linguistic context. In cases where one language is a minority language, frequently the name in this language serves as a marker of identity only within this specific community, while in wider contexts and for communication with speakers of the majority language, the name in the majority language is used exclusively (Aceto 2002: 577-608). Therefore, names are not static, and the names in the inscriptions show one situational facet of identities. Compared with the corpus of runic inscriptions from the Isle of Man, where Norse and Gaelic names are freely mixed (Page 1995: 238-240), names in Orkney appear more uniform in using Norse. This again illustrates Bakhtin's theory on centrifugal and centripetal forces: Orkney, being the closest to the Scandinavian mainland, experiences stronger centripetal forces towards the use of Norse while centrifugal forces become dominant in the Irish Sea with more mixing of languages in naming.

Fig. 2: *OR 1 – Stackrue: a sandstone disc with a carved cross similar to Pictish objects found in Shetland and Portmahomack, with 'koþ' carved in one quadrant. Photo and Copyright: Freund 2019.*

In Orkney, over 50% of inscriptions – 34 out of the 55 (see Appendix) – are in or on ancient monuments, namely Maeshowe and the Ring of Brodgar, with OR 1 (Fig. 2) showing the re-use of a Pictish object with a pre-existing cross-shaped carving. This is not the case to such an extent anywhere else in the Norse world even though occasionally, inscriptions can be found on re-used objects or in older buildings there. This conscious use of the past could signify an attempt to claim the landscape and its heritage as Norse possession. A similar process can be shown for Scotland regarding the establishing of assembly sites. As Sanmark demonstrates, Norse Scotland is similar to Scandinavia and differs from other diaspora locations in that 'thing sites often focused around reused monuments, habitually in the shape of large mounds. These features may have been seen as symbolising the ancestors of the local population and therefore important for the Norse to appropriate in order to claim power and legitimacy to rule' (Sanmark 2017: 219). Crucially, Maeshowe is a likely assembly site (Sanmark 2017: 219) and shows the importance of re-using the past in making Orkney a Norse home both through establishing the Norse legal system and applying the Norse writing system. This re-use of older monuments demonstrates an awareness of the heritage of the landscape and an engagement with the pre-Norse past of Orkney. I would argue that carving runes into pre-existing monuments in the landscape forms a crucial part of stating a claim to this landscape, making a lasting impression in stone in a writing system which is unmistakably Norse. This becomes particularly obvious in Maeshowe where inscriptions discuss the breaking into the monument but also associate it with Norse myth (Barnes 1994). Through the inscriptions, the Norse of the twelfth century both appropriate the Neolithic tomb as connected to their own perceived past and write themselves into the history of the landscape, laying the foundations for claiming a continuing overlordship.

It is crucial that the largest number of runic inscriptions in Orkney post-date the Viking Age. Only decades after the consolidation of kingship in Scotland (cf. Woolf 2007) does it become necessary for elites in Orkney to identify themselves as the epitome of Norse leaders and use the Scandinavian writing system widely. This period also sees the development of the corpus away from 'standardised' memorial inscriptions with few exceptions to a much more diverse application of runes. When looking at the wider political picture of the period, the reasons become more obvious: In 1098, Magnús berfættr Óláfsson of Norway (1073-1103) and Edgar of Scotland (1074-1107) settled the Norwegian-Scottish border in a treaty, and on his expedition to Scotland, Magnús stopped in Orkney with his fleet, resulting in two rebellious Orcadian earls being sent to Norway and the earldom put under direct control of the Norwegian crown until 1102 (Wærdahl 2011: 42-46). This episode established firmer Norwegian control over the earldom and showed the Orcadian elites the potential consequences of perceived disloyalty. Meanwhile, Caithness was held by the Earls of Orkney for the Kingdom of Scotland (Wærdahl 2011: 54), potentially raising additional doubts about their loyalty to Norway. Subsequently, it may have been more necessary than before to show outward loyalty to the Norwegian homeland, and this could be expressed by using the Norse writing system. The increase in rune carving in Orkney in the twelfth century can therefore be regarded as a conscious choice by local elites to outwardly portray a Norse identity, a public rejection of Scottish political and cultural influence.

One as of yet unresolved question is how much runic literacy penetrated everyday activities in Orkney, especially during the climax of rune carving in the mid-twelfth century. Few artefacts from Orkney can be interpreted as pragmatic writing or even trial pieces. The most casual use of runes, in one case even a self-referential joke beginning with the phrase 'this bone was', can be seen on the bone pieces from Earl's Bu. Consequently, the bulk of the corpus is not carved purely for pragmatic communication but to make a deliberate statement. It is impossible to tell if runes were predominantly used epigraphically due to any connotations as a specifically Norse or ancestral script or if preservation conditions in Orkney have prevented any further survival of pragmatic runic writing. As it stands, the corpus appears to support the idea that runes were used in a deliberate way and in specific situations only. In the few cases where the social status of the carvers and their potential audience can be established, the inscriptions appear to be carved by and for an elite. Therefore, while it is justifiable to say that, for this elite, rune carving formed part of the everyday activities taken from the Norse homelands to Orkney, this might not necessarily be true for Norse society in Orkney at every level.

On the whole, the Orcadian corpus of runic inscriptions shows some marked differences to those of mainland Scandinavia. While a quantitative analysis cannot be performed due to varying preservation conditions and differences in sample sizes, some qualitative aspects are striking: Orkney has a far smaller focus on memorial inscriptions; there is currently not a single Orcadian inscription on wood; there is only little evidence for a pragmatic use of runes, and none for their administrative use. While the latter two aspects could potentially be explained by the difficult preservation conditions for organic material in Orkney, with wood being unlikely to be preserved in most cases, and pragmatic writing often using organic media, such as the bone pieces of OR 15 and OR 19, the first aspect requires a different explanation because memorials on stone are among the likeliest inscriptions to be preserved in the archaeological record.

Examining the Orcadian corpus of runic inscriptions shows that at the pinnacle of rune carving in the twelfth century, at least the elites confidently self-identified as Norse. This can be interpreted as a conscious turn against the rising influence of the Scottish crown and a confirmation of the political alignment with Norway. Runic writing constituted an intrinsic part of a wider identification both with a Norse heritage and the contemporaneous Kingdom of Norway. However, this does not imply that the less politically involved inhabitants of Orkney would have identified with the fashion for runes in the same way. Their identities may have been far more localised or mixed, but from a high-status activity, which rune carving appears to have been in Orkney in most cases, it is impossible to draw generalisations about the entire population, even with the relatively rich and varied corpus that has been preserved.

Endnotes

[1] Inscriptions are referenced with signa introduced by Barnes (1994) for Maeshowe, 'OR Barnes' plus number, and Barnes and Page (2006) for non-Maeshowe inscriptions 'OR' plus number.
[2] *Skattland* denotes tributary lands paying tax to the Norwegian crown with a varying degree of direct control through the Norwegian rulers. For details, see Crawford (2013) and Imsen (2014).
[3] For discussion of the standard 'memorial formula', see MacLeod and Mees (2006: 211-213).
[4] For detailed discussions of linguistics and diaspora identities, see for instance Canagarajah and Silberstein (2012) and Bucholtz and Hall (2005).

References

Aceto, M. (2002). 'Ethnic Personal Names and Multiple Identities in Anglophone Caribbean Speech Communities in Latin America', *Language in Society*, 31, pp. 577-608.

Babić, S. (2005). 'Status identity and archaeology', in M. Díaz-Andreu et al. (eds.), *The Archaeology of Identity: Approaches to Gender, Age, Status, Ethnicity and Religion*. London and New York: Routledge, pp. 67-85.

Bakhtin, M. M. (2006). *The Dialogic Imagination: Four Essays*. Austin: University of Texas Press.

Barnes, M. P. (1994). *The Runic Inscriptions of Maeshowe, Orkney*. Uppsala: Institutionen för nordiska språk, Uppsala universitet.

Barnes, M. P. (2015). 'Two Recent Runic Finds from Orkney', *Futhark: International Journal of Runic Studies*, 6, pp. 143-151.

Barnes, M. P. and R. I. Page (2006). *The Scandinavian Runic Inscriptions of Britain*. Uppsala: Institutionen för nordiska språk, Uppsala universitet.

Barrett, J. H. (2015). 'Maritime Societies and the Transformation of the Viking Age and Medieval World', in J. H. Barrett and S. J. Gibbon, (eds.), *Maritime Societies of the Viking and Medieval World*. Leeds: Maney Publishing, pp. 1-13.

Barrett, J. H. and M. P. Richards (2004). 'Identity, Gender, Religion and Economy: New Isotope and Radiocarbon Evidence for Marine Resource Intensification in Early Historic Orkney, Scotland, UK', *European Journal of Archaeology*, 7, pp. 249-271.

Batey, C. E. and C. D. Morris (1989). 'Excavations at the Earl's Bu, Orphir, Orkney, 1988'. University of Durham and University of Newcastle upon Tyne: Archaeological Reports, 1988/1989, 47 - 50

Bucholtz, M. and K. Hall (2005), 'Identity and Interaction: A Sociocultural Linguistic Approach', *Discourse Studies*, 7 (4-5), pp. 585-614.

Canagarajah, S. and S. Silberstein (2012). 'Diaspora Identities and Language', *Journal of Language, Identity and Education*, 11 (2), pp. 81-84.

Crawford, B. E. (2013). *The Northern Earldoms: Orkney and Caithness from AD 870 to 1470.* Edinburgh: Birlinn.

Curtin, P. D. (1984). *Cross-cultural Trade in World History.* Cambridge: Cambridge University Press.

Freund, A. and R. Ljosland (2019). 'Modern Rune Carving in Northern Scotland', *Futhark: International Journal of Runic Studies*, 8, pp. 127-150.

Hall, S. (1990). 'Cultural Identity and Diaspora', in Rutherford, J. (ed.), *Identity: Community, Culture, Difference.* London: Lawrence and Wishart, pp. 222-237.

Hull, R. (2007). *Scottish Mammals.* Edinburgh: Birlinn.

Imer, L. M. (2017). *Peasants and Prayers: The Inscriptions of Norse Greenland.* Odense: University Press of Southern Denmark.

Imsen, S. (ed.) (2014). *Rex Insularum: The King Of Norway And His "Skattlands" As A Political System c. 1260 - c. 1450.* Bergen: Fagbokforlaget.

Jesch, J. (2015). *The Viking Diaspora.* Abingdon: Routledge.

Kalra, V., R. K. Kalhon, and J. Hutynuk (2005). *Diaspora and Hybridity.* London: Sage Publications.

Lamb, R. G. (1993). 'Carolingian Orkney and its Transformation', in Batey, C. E., Jesch, J. and Morris, C. D. (eds.), *The Viking Age in Caithness, Orkney and the North Atlantic.* Edinburgh: Edinburgh University Press, pp. 260-271.

Ljosland, R. (forthcoming). 'Runic Spindle Whorl Recently Found in Orkney', *Futhark: International Journal of Runic Studies*, 9.

MacLeod, M. and B. Mees (2006). *Runic Amulets and Magic Objects.* Woodbridge: Boydell.

Marwick, H. (1952). *Orkney Farm-Names.* Kirkwall: W. R. Mackintosh.

Morris, C. D. (1989). *The Birsay Bay Project*. Durham: University of Durham, Dept. of Archaeology.

Page, R. I. (1995). *Runes and Runic Inscriptions: Collected Essays on Anglo-Saxon and Viking Runes*. Woodbridge: Boydell Press.

Samnordisk Runtextdatabas (2018). Uppsala: Uppsala Universitet.

Sanmark, A. (2017). *Viking Law and Order: Places and Rituals of Assembly in the Medieval North*. Edinburgh: Edinburgh University Press.

Sindbæk, S. M. (2015). 'Steatite Vessels and the Viking Diaspora: Migrants, Travellers and Cultural Change in Early Medieval Britain and Ireland', in J. H. Barrett and S. J. Gibbon (eds.), *Maritime Societies of the Viking and Medieval World*. Leeds: Maney Publishing, pp. 198-218.

Steenholt Olesen, R. (2010). 'Runic Amulets from Medieval Denmark', *Futhark: International Journal for Runic Studies*, 1, pp. 161-176.

Thomson, W. P. L. (2012). 'Orkney Skaill-names', *Northern Scotland*, 3, pp. 1-15.

Thomson, W. P. L. (2008). *The New History of Orkney*. Edinburgh: Birlinn.

Williams, H. (1990). *Åsrunan: användning och ljudvärde i runsvenska steninskrifter*. Uppsala: Institutionen för nordiska språk, Uppsala Universitet.

Woolf, A. (2007). *From Pictland to Alba: 789-1070*. Edinburgh: Edinburgh University Press.

Wærdahl, R. B. (2011). *The Incorporation and Integration of the King's Tributary Lands into the Norwegian Realm c. 1195-1397*. Leiden: Brill.

Yalden, D. W. (1999). *The History of British Mammals*. London: T. and A. D. Poyser.

Appendix: Runic inscriptions from Orkney (outside Maeshowe)

Signum	Inscription	Find spot	Material
OR 1	k(o)(þ) <f>a <h>(n) r	Broch of Stackrue, Sandwick	Sandstone disc
OR 2 - modern	(n) (u)(k)(f)/(t)(k)(f) <(i)>{(K)}----	Unstan cairn	Stone
OR 3	--ka---r (r)es- run--	Stromness	Steatite spindle whorl
OR 4	<n>r<o><(i)(n)>	Ring of Brodgar	Stone/Monolith
OR 5 - lost	[<o>]	Ring of Brodgar	Stone
OR 6	--------- ----- filibus ra^nru	Brough of Birsay	Stone
OR 7	<im> -	Brodgar farm	Stone
OR 8	× ------ × (r)(a)-(s)-- ...	Brough of Birsay	Stone
OR 9	...----- ----- --...	Brough of Birsay	Stone
OR 10	ik ir girgia koþ (l)(i)uf (:) s-... ...	Orphir	Stone
OR 11	fuþork-	Brough of Birsay	Bear's tooth
OR 12	---	Westness, Rousay	Antler needle
OR 13 - modern	§A <iba> §B r-r	Skara Brae	Stone
OR 14	þorst--n (æ)inar(s) (s)unr : ræist : ru-ar þ(i)sar	Tuquoy, Westray	Stone
OR 15	...-ta : bain : uas · (i)-(u)--...	Earl's Bu, Orphir	Bone

OR 16	...	Church ruin, Brough of Birsay	Stone
OR 17	...n × in : osk(a)-- : r... ...	Litte Isegarth, Sanday	Stone
OR 18	§A þurfinr : r---- ----- : --n- : --... ... §B ...	Skaill Home Farm, Sandwick	Stone
OR 19	...----ssr...	Earl's Bu, Orphir	Assemblage of bone pieces
OR 20	...þ--br-(u)...	Breckness	Stone
OR 21	§A ... §B ...	Brough of Deerness	Copper alloy pin
OR 22	§A ...-rasab-... §B ...y-iþik-...	Quoys, Deerness	Folded lead plate
OR 23	... -(s) in silis| |santifi(t)s(i) tor ÷	Naversdale, Orphir	Stone
OR 24	...utharkhniastl...	Burray	Bone spindle whorl

VISUAL HOMES

Skagen: A Utopia of the North?

Jan D. Cox

This chapter examines why in the nineteenth century Skagen became the most important artists' colony in Denmark, and arguably the most important in Europe. It analyses the factors that contributed to this, and emphasises the importance of the Møller and Brøndum families in providing a haven for artists. After providing a brief history of the genesis of the colony, the core argument centres on the social divisions that existed in the town, and particularly whether the fisherfolk were exploited by the artists or benefitted from their presence. The arguments put forward by leading Skagen art historian Mette Bøgh Jensen are discussed. In Danish terms, the town was seen as a remote Northern outpost; this perception altered during the century as transport links improved.

The fact that this community was isolated and depicted as possessing a wholesome lifestyle leads to comparisons with the fictionalised inhabitants of *Shangri-La* (James Hilton, 1933) and *Utopia* (Thomas More, 1516). As discussed later, it is the latter that invites us to consider existence in Skagen in similar terms: open doors, lack of privacy, lack of material possessions, evening classes, a rural (non-industrial) economy, accessible by water, distant from other settlements. In *Utopia*, settlements must be at least 24 miles from each other – Skagen is 25 miles from Frederikshavn.

The town of Skagen is situated on a narrow peninsula at the very north of Denmark, with the North Sea on one side and the Baltic on the other. Until the railway arrived in 1890, it was a remote fishing village, possessing neither road access nor harbour. There were two methods of arrival, the first being a five-hour journey by mail coach along the beach from Frederikshavn, which had received its own railway link to the rest of Denmark in 1871. This journey was dependent on travel conditions and the Finnish painter Hanna Rönneberg described it as being 'like riding in flour, up dune and down dune' (Lübbren 2001: 147). This experience is well illustrated in Carl Locher's painting *Ageposten* (*The Mail Coach*,1885; Skagens Museum). The alternative was to arrive by boat, with at the end a transfer to a rowing boat and then your person and your luggage carried ashore by fishermen clad in waders.

Fig. 1. *Martinus Rørbye, [Et skib på Skagens strand. Der er tale om Ann af Sunderland, forlist ved Skagens Rev, 28. november 1846] A Ship on Skagen's Beach [The Ann of Sunderland, foundered November 28, 1846], 1847, oil on canvas, 37 x 55.5 cm, private collection. Copyright: Wikimedia Commons.*

The first painter to arrive in the fishing community there was Martinus Rørbye in 1833, when Skagen had a population of around 1200. He revisited in 1847. The people lived on fishing, and a bit of hunting, but extra income was provided by the numerous wrecks that occurred. A number of merchants acted as receivers of wrecks and the waters were highly treacherous, as the *Ann* from Sunderland (Fig. 1) – probably carrying coal – found out (Krohg and Garrett 2017: 217). Rørbye painted the scene the year after the wreck occurred as salvage operations were underway.

The most significant result of Rørbye's second visit was the painting *Mænd af Skagen en sommeraften i godt vejr* (*Men of Skagen on a Summer Evening in Good Weather*, 1848; Statens Museum for Kunst, Copenhagen). We see different social classes depicted here. Working men are relaxing after a day's work, talking, and enjoying a pipe. However, the businessman and salvage operator Jakob Andersen appears vigilant despite the calm sea beyond (Berman 2007: 137-139). This picture is an early indication of the different roles of the working class and an entrepreneurial business class in Skagen, one able to relax and the other always alert for the chance of a profit. Rørbye was by now professor at the Royal Academy in Copenhagen, but died the year he painted this picture. It was exhibited at the annual Charlottenborg exhibition in Copenhagen, and bought by the new King of Denmark, Frederick VII (ruled 1848-1863) giving publicity to Skagen as a location.

It is worth summarising here the factors that made Skagen an archetypal nineteenth-century artists' colony; the colony's peak years were concentrated in the late 1870s and the 1880s. The majority of the factors below were shared with other European artists' colonies such as St. Ives, Grez-sur-Loing or Volendam.[1] A common pursuit was the search for locations that provided exceptional light.

Firstly, the location, in that Skagen was semi-accessible. The major part of the journey by land (particularly from 1871) or sea was relatively straightforward, but then presented a final difficult stage that gave the traveller a sense of great achievement upon arrival. In her book on artists' colonies, Nina Lübbren describes such exertions as 'a physical rite of passage into the pre-modern' (Lübbren 2001: 147). This difficult stretch also deterred casual visitors and made the location more exclusive.

Secondly, the setting. Skagen has a coastal setting (in fact two coasts) where the sea could provide a backdrop for pictures. Both artists and their patrons were attracted by landscapes that contained water; in France, south of Paris, this was a major factor in artists leaving the relatively dry Barbizon area for nearby Grez-sur-Loing, where the river and attendant bridge provided an aquatic vista.

Thirdly, accommodation. As in other artists' colonies mentioned above, the inn (Brøndums Hotel) played a pivotal role as a communal centre for lodging, eating, drinking, meeting, socialising, and even educating.

Fourthly, motifs. In the second half of the nineteenth century there was a move away from the Romanticism of the previous generation of artists, and towards a natural and unsentimental depiction of the lives of working people. These were rural folk, not urban, and thus seen to be uncorrupted by the material temptations of city life. They were far less afflicted by the squalor and disease that often accompanied urban working people at a time of booming populations, overcrowded housing and growing industrialisation. Fishermen and their families provided excellent motifs as they were seen as strong, hard-working, heroic figures, battling against the sea. The painters depicted their intimate lives and deaths: Among the many motifs captured by Christian Krohg, Anna and Michael Ancher, P. S. Krøyer and Oscar Björck were the fisherfolk plucking gulls, sleeping, whittling on a stick, heading for sea, launching boats, hauling nets, hauling lifeboats, and coping with the tragedy of death by drowning.

Finally, a form of celebrity endorsement. As mentioned above, in 1848 the King bought a Skagen picture. Back in 1830 the little-known Hans Christian Andersen had met Rørbye[2] on a voyage to Jutland, which he described as stretching 'between the German Ocean and the Baltic, until it ends at Skagen in a reef of quicksands' (Andersen in Berman 2007: 137). In 1859, the by now famous Andersen went to Skagen itself, his arrival apparently precipitating the birth of the hotel proprietor's daughter Anna Brøndum, famous later as the artist Anna Ancher (Andersen arrived on 17 August 1859, and she was born on 18 August). Andersen returned to Copenhagen and before the year was out published 'En Historie fra Klitterne' ('Tale of the Dunes'), telling of the Skagen church that had been buried by drifting sands in 1775, and a travelogue, *Skagen*, which anticipated its future role: '[...] this far away place, this desert between two foaming oceans, the town with neither streets or alleys [...]. If you are a painter follow us here because you will find a profusion of subjects to paint. Here are scenes to inspire poetry [...]. Skagen is indeed worth a visit' (Andersen cited in Berman 2007: 138).

Skagen might still have remained only moderately exposed, were it not for the arrival in 1882 of P. S. Krøyer, an internationally successful artist with the drive to establish Skagen as a meeting place for a select group of artists and literary figures.

I now want to return to another social class in Skagen, a group one might describe as a business elite. They differed from other local inhabitants in that they were wealthier, much better educated, had less physically demanding work, had regular contact with – and made visits to – Copenhagen, and were also far more cosmopolitan in their outlook. They were landowners, merchants, and innkeepers. Key to this in Skagen are the Møller and Brøndum families.

Søren Pedersen 'Møller'	m.	Kirsten Eskildsen
(b. Mygdal 1801 d. Skagen 1876)		(b. Skagen 1804 d. Skagen 1886)

6 children including:

Ane Sørensdatter Møller	and	Laurits (Lars) Sørensen Møller
b. Skagen 1826 d. Skagen 1916		b. Skagen 1830 d. Hjørring 1875
1847 m. Erik Brøndum (1820-1890)		1850s m. Caroline Holm (1819-1883)
6 children, including:		4 children including:

Anna Brøndum (Painter)	Martha Møller	Johanne Henriette Møller
b. Skagen **1859** d. Skagen 1935	b. **1860** d.1929	b. Øster Thirup **1859** d. 1881
1880 m. Michael Ancher	**1880** m. Viggo Johansen	**1880** m. Karl Madsen
(1849-1927) Painter	(1851-1935) Painter	(1855-1938) Painter, Critic

Fig. 2. *Simplified family tree of the Skagen-based cousins Anna Ancher (1859-1935), Martha Møller (1860-1929) and Johanne Henriette Møller (1859-1881), and their marriages in 1880 to three painters.*

In 1839, Erik Brøndum's mother inherited a merchant's farm in Skagen, and summoned Erik home to help her. Erik married Ane Møller in 1847, and in 1850 they took over the farm. In May 1858, the couple were given permission to convert the farm to a guesthouse, just in time for – or perhaps precipitating – Hans Christian Andersen's arrival the following year. Meanwhile, in 1853, Ane's brother Lars Møller bought a farm near Hjørring about fifty kilometres south-west of Skagen. Thus, both the Brøndums and the Møllers were property owners. Møller's two daughters did not attend the local school but travelled each day to Hjørring in their own horse-drawn carriage (Svanholm 2004: 9). Between them the brother and sister had ten children with their respective spouses, but two of Lars Møller's four children died within eleven days of each other before the age of five, leaving two sisters Henriette (b. 1859) and Martha (b. 1860), who were both to marry artists.

In 1871, the railway link as far as Frederikshavn was completed, and sixteen-year-old Karl Madsen visited his uncle Johan Pohlmann Thorsøe who was a prominent citizen there. Madsen then travelled on to Skagen, where he was well-received at Brøndums lodgings by Ane (Svanholm 2004: 54). Holger Drachmann, later a famous poet but then primarily a marine artist, also paid his first visit to Skagen that year, and published an article in which he declared Skagen 'an eldorado for artists' (Berman 2007: 141). Madsen, both of whose parents were artists, went to the Royal Danish Academy in Copenhagen in 1873, and in 1874 persuaded fellow student Michael Ancher to go to Skagen with him; Ancher loved the place. The Brøndum lodgings had been very badly damaged by fire in January 1874 and afterwards a new larger main wing was added with family rooms, a tavern, a grocer's shop, and stables. The garden house was retained. Then a tall two-storey building was built including ten guest rooms, initiating the Brøndums Hotel (Svanholm 2004: 21). Meanwhile Lars Møller had decided that farming was not for him, and brought his wife and two daughters from Øster Thirup outside Hjørring to the garden house in the grounds of his sister's inn in Skagen (Svanholm 2004: 9).

1875 was a key year in Skagen. Not only did Lars Møller die in April aged forty-four, but that summer, his two daughters Martha and Henriette, and their cousin Anna Brøndum, all aged around fifteen, plus another older close friend Helene Christensen, hid behind a dune to witness the arrival of another painter friend of Ancher and Madsen, the 'unusually handsome and likeable' Viggo Johansen (Svanholm 2004: 9).[3] That summer the three young cousins all became secretly engaged to the three older painters from Copenhagen (Svanholm 2004: 10). All three girls then went to the capital, and Anna Brøndum was given tuition there for three years by the traditionalist landscape artist Vilhelm Kyhn at his Tegneskolen for Kvinder (Drawing School for Women).

In the space of ten weeks in 1880, Anna, Martha, and Henriette married Michael, Viggo, and Karl (see Fig. 2). Later P. S. Krøyer had a relationship with the fourth friend, Helene Christensen. So the male 'incomer' painters either married – or had relationships with – girls of the higher social class in Skagen. Class boundaries seemed very strong as there is no apparent recorded mention of a relationship at any time between either the fishing people and the Copenhagen painters, or the local bourgeois business people. (All translations from Danish below are by Jan Cox based on an initial translation organised by Mary O'Neill [2014]).

Leading Skagen art historian Mette Bøgh Jensen said of the painters and fisherfolk: 'De to grupper havde i virkeligheden meget lidt med hinanden at gøre [...]. De to grupper var som forholdet mellem arbejdsgiver og arbejdstager' (Jensen 2005: 106) (In reality, the two groups had very little to do with each other – relations were like that between employer and employee)

Was the lack of 'suitable' spouses of the right class one of the reasons why none of Anna's three sisters and two brothers married, including innkeeper and artists' friend Degn Brøndum, or were there religious or other reasons involved? Michael Jacobs relates how in 1883 in Skagen on the birthday of Norwegian painter Eilif Peterssen, a dance was arranged, but there were only two women present, Anna's sister Agnes and her close friend, Krøyer's putative girlfriend Helene Christensen. At this point the local fishermen with wives and daughters were invited in, and a great deal of dancing ensued (Jacobs 1985: 101).

In the spring of 1880, Michael Ancher's Skagen picture *Vil han Klare Pynten* (*Will he Clear the Point?*, 1879; Amalienborg Palace, Copenhagen) was exhibited at Charlottenborg in Copenhagen and purchased by King Christian IX (ruled 1863-1906). When Anna married Michael that August, her old Copenhagen painting tutor Vilhelm Kyhn told her that it was now time for her to throw her paintbox into the sea (Berman 2007: 150; Svanholm 2004: 56); in the nineteenth century, it was expected that after marriage a woman should devote herself entirely to husband and children. A well-publicised example of this is the case of Edma Morisot, who was the sister of leading Impressionist Berthe Morisot, and sacrificed the career she loved for the needs of her family after she married a naval officer.[4]

Anna's picture *Lars Gaihede snitter en Pind* (*Lars Gaihede Whittling a Stick*, 1880; Skagens Museum) had been exhibited at Charlottenborg that year also. The A B signature in the bottom right corner informs us that the picture was painted prior to her marriage, but she gaily ignored the advice she had received from Kyhn. That same fisherman, now in his mid-seventies, had been drawn by Martinus Rørbye thirty-three years previously as *Fiskeren Lars Gaihede* (*The Fisherman Lars Gaihede*, 1847; Skagens Museum), illustrative of the narrow percentage of fishermen and their families who posed for artists. In 1881 a tragedy occurred when Anna's cousin Henriette Madsen died in childbirth. Her husband Karl gave up painting and later became Denmark's leading art critic and curator, as well as the first director of Skagens Museum in 1928.

Back in 1879, Michael Ancher had been upset that some of the foreign painters in Skagen – Norwegians, Swedes, a German[5] – had been 'stimulating company' for his future wife Anna. In October 1879 Anna wrote to her cousin Martha 'there has been a lot of bother, but then again so much clarification, [...] now I hope things will be alright' (Svanholm 2004: 49-50). Michael felt that other artists were muscling in on his own adopted territory. Ancher again showed how sensitive he was to other artists inhabiting Skagen when, in 1882, P. S. Krøyer met the married Anchers and Johansens in Vienna, and decided to visit Skagen that summer. In previous painting locations, Krøyer had the clever idea of painting an indoor and an outdoor picture at the same time, thus he wasn't weather dependent. When he arrived at Skagen in June it was wet, so without further ado he began sketching in the Brøndums shop, resulting in *I købmandens bod*, *når der ikke fiskes* (*At the Victuallers when there is no fishing*,1882; Hirschsprung Collection, Copenhagen), complete with Michael Ancher's brother-in-law Degn Brøndum at the end of the shop counter. Michael Ancher was not happy and in November wrote to Krøyer: 'You paint my parents-in-law's shop, you could scarcely come much closer [...] it was an attack on a place that was mine, it reminds one of the rich man who had many sheep, but slaughtered the poor man's only lamb' (Ancher cited in Svanholm 2004: 66).

There were further problems with Krøyer's outdoor picture *Fiskere trækker Vaad ved Skagens Nordstrand. Sildig Eftermiddag* (*Fishermen hauling in their Nets, Skagen North Beach*, 1882-1883; Skagens Museum). In September he wrote to his mother complaining that the fishermen were too busy fishing to act as models for his pictures, and he was thus wasting valuable time (Cox 2014: 117), and in November a further complaint from Michael Ancher against Krøyer: 'there are probably some 500 fishermen in Skagen, and of these I have perhaps painted 20. You come and you paint the very same 20, or at least 10 of the 20' (Ancher in Svanholm 2004: 66). The reliability and exclusivity of the fishermen/models caused problems and friction between the artists.

Let us subject to analysis some of the statements made by Mette Bøgh Jensen in her excellently-researched chapter on 'The Relationship between Fishermen and Artists' (Jensen 2005: 106-151). I have the greatest respect for Jensen, but want to put forward some alternative suggestions and act as 'devil's advocate', with the overarching idea that the situation may have been somewhat more nuanced than she suggests. (All quotes are from Jensen 2005). She proposes that relations were:

> som forholdet mellem arbejdsgiver og arbejdstager. (106) Kunstnernes beskrivelser af deres forhold til lokalbefolkningen bærer stærkt præg af en manglende evne eller et manglende

ønske om at sætte sig ind i de vilkår, som befolkningen levede under. (108)

(like that between employer and employee. [...] The artists' descriptions of their relationships with the local population are highly marked by an inability or a lack of desire [by the painters] to acquaint themselves with the conditions in which people lived.)

We know that the lives of working fisherfolk and urban, educated artists are very different. I propose that the fisherfolk didn't want to get to know the artists as friends, as they had so little in common. The fishing people's conversation revolved around fishing and boats, the painters around painting and art.

Similarly, it is suggested '[a]t kunstnerne i virkeligheden foretrak at være sammen med andre kunstnere eller repræsentanter for borgerskabet' (111) (that artists in fact preferred to be with other artists or representatives of the bourgeoisie).

This seems unsurprising to me; we all tend to socialise with the people we have most in common with. It is further suggested that 'Fiskerne forstod også at udnytte kunstnernes tilstedeværelse... for eksempel ved at drikke dus med kunstnerne på kunstnernes regning' (111) (Fishermen also understood how to utilise the artists' presence [...] for example by drinking with artists at the artists' expense).

This appears unproblematic to me, as the artists were in the fortunate financial position whereby they could afford to entertain.

It is also proposed that 'beskrivelserne af loppebidene [...] som kunstnerne måtte udholde, fungerede samtidig som en iscenesættelse af autenticiteten' (110) (that descriptions of fleabites [...] which the artists had to endure, functioned [...] as a staging of authenticity).

There are parallels with the situation in St. Ives following the death of the artist Alfred Wallis, where Adrian Stokes (1902-1972)[6] cleared out the old mariner's cottage 'at the cost of more flea bites than he cared to remember' (Mullins 1967: 44). My suggestion is that the artists would rather have had no flea bites and less authenticity.

It is also stated that in Skagen '[m]an kan som fremmed for eksempel gå inn i hvilket hus man vil og se seg om i deres stuer' (Christian Krohg cited in Jensen 2005: 108) (one could as a stranger, for example, go into whichever [fisherfolk] house you want and watch them in their living rooms). Krohg's words were expanded upon: 'A stranger, for example, can enter any house and poke around in their living rooms. They make no fuss, continue eating, sleeping or dressing entirely undisturbed. One is immediately acquainted with them' (Krohg and Garrett: 2017: 218). Krohg makes the point that these people do not share our modern notions of privacy. Fjågesund and Symes recount how in nineteenth-century Norway, British travellers were amazed at how the young female maids would wander into their rooms and completely ignore their state of dress or lack of it (Fjågesund and Symes 2003: 217). The fishing people had a totally different concept of privacy from that which we know today, and being observed by artists in intimate situations would not have caused them concern.

More importantly, it is noted that '[f]lere af Krohgs værker [...] viser familiens medlemmer i sårbare og intime situationer, blandt andet mens de sover' (Jensen 2005: 108) (several of Krohg's works [...] show family members in *vulnerable* [my emphasis] and intimate situations, including while they are sleeping).

Indeed, some of these pictures are intimate. From the available evidence, my belief is that these people were not coerced into this, or exploited, or that they resented it. They had the option to tell the artist to go away. They would certainly have been pleased with the payment they received. It is surely significant that only a small percentage of fisher families were painted (as explained by Michael Ancher earlier), presumably those who viewed it as being to their advantage. I suggest that we need to consider the notion of personal privacy as it existed in Skagen at that time. We must also think about the much-discussed question of the artists' motives: 'Kunstnerne opholdt sig ikke i kunstnerkolonien for at *dokumentere* livets gang, men for at *male* det' (Jensen 2005: 127, emphasis original) (The artists stayed in the artist colony not to *document* life as it was lived, but to *paint* it).

This raises the whole notion of the purpose of art and reminds us of Walter Benjamin's criticism of German photographers whom he accused of taking images of abject poverty and making them into objects of enjoyment (Benjamin 1982: 215). Life was certainly hard in Skagen, but everyone appeared relatively well-nourished in comparison with their urban counterparts. Compare the images of these fisherfolk with Harald Slott-Møller's [*Fattigfolk. I dødens venteværelse* (*The Poor: The Waiting Room of Death*, 1888; Statens Museum for Kunst, Copenhagen) in which the urban poor of Copenhagen await their end. Very few European painters, whether Naturalist or Impressionist, were interested in portraying social issues at this time; painters had to live, and patrons weren't keen on depictions of a (as they saw it) threatening proletariat.[7] It is also proposed that 'Ancher [...] iscenesatte fiskerne som helte [...] mens Krøyer i sine værker af fiskerne snarere interesserede sig for forskellige lysvirkninger' (Jensen 2005: 116) ([Michael] Ancher [...] staged the fishermen as heroes; Krøyer, on the other hand, was interested in the different lighting effects in his representations of fishermen).

Krøyer had but one priority in his art – the capture of light. The representation of it was his entire *raison d'être*. He painted a picture in Italy in 1880, *Italienske Landsbyhattemagere* (*The Italian Village Hatters*, 1880; Hirschsprung Collection, Copenhagen) that was perceived in Copenhagen to be political, though his priorities as he told his mother were:

> The lighting, the contrasts between the characters of the various naked bodies, the father's lean, characteristic body and the children's – one skinny, the other round and plump. It is a pure treat to paint. (Krøyer, 15 August 1880, quoted in Saabye 2011a: 200-201)

There was nothing political in Krøyer's intent, but it wasn't seen that way back in Denmark, where it was construed as an attack on the bourgeoisie. The Danish periodical *Højskolebladet* doubted whether 'such figments of the imagination' existed at all and whether 'yon human baboon with his dripping nose and the filthy kids were a picture of reality' (Monrad and Hornung 2002: 2). Krøyer was very upset and did not paint anything again that could be interpreted as being political. Note his unrealistically pristine depiction of *Fra Burmeister & Wains jernstøberi* (*The Iron Foundry, Burmeister and Wain*, 1885; Statens Museum for Kunst), in which manual labour appears safe, clean and undemanding. Krøyer was criticised then for being too political, whereas today, the priority he gave to capturing of the effects of light as against social concerns is scrutinised. Finally, it is suggested that 'det var problematisk for kunstnerne at afbilde sig selv sammen med deres modeller, fordi det afslørede, at det var tale om en opstillet situation' (Jensen 2005: 141) (it was problematic for the artists to depict themselves with their models because it revealed that it was a contrived situation). I would counter that very few artists included themselves in their pictures with their models, unless it was a deliberate contrivance on their part.[8]

Ancher eventually became friends with Krøyer, who said 'Skagen is an excellent place for painters […] we form quite a pleasant little company, Ancher, Drachmann and I, neither too few nor too many' (Svanholm 2004: 73). We can describe this group as a sociable elite. But after the railway link arrived in 1890, Krøyer complained that 'the place is so overrun with travellers in the summer months that the happy old atmosphere of artist life at Brøndums hotel has become impossible' (Krøyer in Saabye 1990: 152); ironically, some of these tourists would have been attracted to Skagen by Krøyer's own pictures.

It would be fair to describe the painters at Skagen as pan-Nordic. Nina Lübbren records seventy-five artists and analyses the visitors to be ninety-four per cent Scandinavian, mostly Danish but with some prominent Norwegians and Swedes, and also one Finn (Lübbren 2001: 174).[9] In 1908, the writer and cultural critic Georg Brandes said 'the entire company sat from morning to evening around the table in Brøndums [...] eating, drinking, debating, discussing, contradicting, damning. A couple of times a day they went for a swim' (cited in Svanholm 2004: 75-76). The former group of activities is represented well by Krøyer's *Ved Frokosten* (*Artists' Luncheon at Brøndum's Hotel*, 1883; Skagens Museum), but there is no illustration of artists swimming at Skagen.

Let us consider the notion of Skagen as a Northern outpost of Utopia, by making comparisons with the famous sixteenth-century model community. Interestingly, in Thomas More's *Utopia* there are no locks on the doors of the houses: 'Who so will may go in, for there is nothing within the houses that is private or any man's own' (More 1978 [1516]: 60-61). More's description resonates with the lack of material possessions and lack of concept of privacy of the Skagen fisherfolk. Also, in *Utopia*, people are encouraged to spend their leisure time in learning: 'A great multitude of every sort of people, both men and women, go to hear lectures' (More 1978: 65). In Skagen they had an evening academy. Apparently, on special occasions such as the 'store Gala-Academi-Dage' (great Gala-Academy-Days), 'et malerisk og decorativt Moment' (a picturesque and decorative Moment) was achieved by 'at forpligte Fiskerne til [...] at møde frem i Olietøj, Sydvest osv.' (Jensen 2005: 112) (requiring the fishermen to...turn up wearing their oilskins, sou'westers, etc.). This may seem exploitative, but the fishermen were compensated by the liquor they were provided with, and there is no evidence that they disliked the experience. Indeed, there were numerous celebrations at Skagen – arrivals, departures, holidays, birthdays, and anniversaries. Much of this was organised by Krøyer, firstly because he could afford the bill and also because he could paint with such ease and rapidity that he had plenty of free time. In his picture *Oscar Björck og Eilif Peterssen maler Georg Brandes* (*Oscar Björck and Eilif Peterssen painting portraits of Georg Brandes*, 1883; Randers Kunstmuseum), Krøyer depicts how he got tired of waiting for Oscar Björck and Eilif Peterssen to finish painting Brandes – he had completed his own portrait of the writer in two hours – and began a pastel of the other two artists.

It is further suggested that the fishing work at Skagen is not shown 'som hårdt og opslidende' (Jensen 2005: 132) (as hard and gruelling). An abundance of fish is equated with hard work, comparing the meagre quantity of fish in *Fangsten deles* (*Dividing the Catch*, 1885; Skagens Museum) by Viggo Johansen and idyllic scenery in Krøyer's *Fiskere trækker Vaad ved Skagens Nordstrand. Sildig Eftermiddag* (*Fishermen hauling in their Nets, Skagen North Beach*, 1882-83; Skagens Museum), with a bounty of fish in Percy Craft's *Tucking a School of Pilchards* (1897; Penlee House, Penzance). Johansen's surroundings are described as 'øde og mennesketomme' (Jensen 2005: 131) (desolate and deserted); in the Craft picture, according to Jensen, the explicit hard work is exemplified by some of the older fishermen having to take a break (Jensen 2005: 132-133). While I agree that depictions of Skagen fishermen do not emphasise the dangers that were inherent in the job, I wonder how practical it would be for painters to go off on long fishing expeditions in treacherous waters, perhaps tied to the mast in a storm as Turner was rumoured to have done (an apocryphal tale?).[10] However, as Newlyn had a harbour, it was practical for many people to head out in their boats and help with the catch; Craft's pilchard haul is very close to land. This would not have been possible at Skagen until the harbour was built in 1904-1907.

Again, we must ask, should artists work as artists or as investigative reporters, exemplified by the Danish-born Jacob Riis, who utilised his camera in New York in the 1880s to expose social inequities – a far more instantaneous and effective way to capture poverty where a political outcome was desired. What does seem shocking is that Anna Ancher, who had grown up among the fishermen's families, described the scene of six drowned young fishermen as 'storartet, tragisk og smukt' (Ancher cited in Jensen 2005: 126) (magnificent, tragic, and beautiful). Was death so normal in this place that she saw only a painterly subject? One is reminded of the fashion for dead Victorian children to be photographed as a type of *memento mori* (Bell 2016); a reminder that early death was commonplace in those times and would eventually claim us all.

In terms of size, content and length of completion, two major Skagen paintings of the 1880s stand out. *Hip, hip, hurra! Kunstnerfest på Skagen* (*Hip! Hip! Hurrah! Artists' Party*, 1885-1888; Göteborgs Konstmuseum) features a celebration of artists in Skagen by Krøyer, and *En Barnedaab* (*A Christening*: 1883-1888; Ribe Kunstmuseum, [Fig 3]) by Michael Ancher features the christening of the Anchers' only child, Helga. Both paintings caused many headaches for the painters because the original models kept disappearing.[11] The final compositions include only four shared characters: Krøyer, and Michael, Anna and Helga Ancher.[12] Michael, particularly, altered the people in his composition many times. The 'cap-mother' behind Anna Ancher was in 1887 Helene Christensen, then in 1888 perhaps a Møller cousin of Anna's, then in the final version a girl from Skagen, Ms Arvidsen (Nielsen-Bergqvist 2018: 49-53). The depiction of light is crucial to both works. These pictures show a unity, both joyous and solemn, that was not to be borne out by events.

Fig. 3. *Michael Ancher, En Barnedaab (A Christening, 1883-88), oil on canvas, 186 x 250 cm, Ribe Kunstmuseum. Far left: Michael Ancher, Mr Mariager. Middle row: Marianne Stokes, P. S. Krøyer, John Brøndum. Front row: Anna Ancher (with doll representing Helga) and Ms Arvidsen. Copyright: Wikimedia Commons.*

Krøyer, the Anchers, and Viggo Johansen went to Paris for the 1889 *Exposition Universelle* where they all won major awards (Cox 2014: 327). Krøyer arrived back in Copenhagen from Skagen in October 1888 and left for Paris on 16 November (Saabye 2011b: 330). A month later Krøyer again met the beautiful Marie Triepcke — she had posed for him earlier in the painting *En Duet* (*A Duet*, 1887; Statens Museum for Kunst, Copenhagen) — and by May 1889, at the time of the opening of the *Exposition*, they had become engaged. This meant that Krøyer had forsaken Helene Christensen – 'Lille' as he affectionately called her (Loerges 1977: 33) – and left her behind in Skagen when the artists went to Paris.

What actually happened is not straightforward. Michael Jacobs writes about Krøyer's picture *Hip, hip, hurra!* and says that 'In the intervening years since 1884 Helene had been made pregnant by Krøyer and [...] had travelled to America where she suffered a miscarriage' (Jacobs 1985: 105). However, Margrethe Loerges explains that it was after the end of their affair (in the summer of 1888) that Christensen 'travelled to America with the help of the Anchers, where she gave birth to a boy who died' (Loerges 1977: 33). More recent scholarship by Lise Svanholm states that after teaching and tutoring jobs in Kalundborg and Copenhagen, Christensen emigrated to the USA at the beginning of 1891 and by December of that year was in Texas (Svanholm 2006: 60-61), all this long after she had last seen Krøyer in the summer of 1888, and therefore unconnected with a pregnancy. Lise Svanholm also mentions a letter of 1888 in which Martha Johansen knows of a Christensen pregnancy, but Krøyer and Ancher do not (Svanholm 2006: 61). Krøyer's inclusion of Christensen in *Hip! Hip! Hurrah!*, exhibited in Gothenburg in the autumn of 1888, backs up the idea that he wasn't aware of her condition. Martha Johansen was particularly disgusted with Krøyer, as she felt he had betrayed her childhood friend, though Johansen herself had found the needy and sickly Christensen somewhat of a burden (Svanholm 2004: 120-121). From these different sources, one can conclude that Christensen did have a pregnancy, but that this was either immediately prior to, or at the time of, her parting from Krøyer in the summer of 1888, and that it was not related to her trip to America in early 1891. It seems likely that there was either an abortion or a miscarriage, as the fate of the child is unknown (Svanholm 2006: 60-61).

Martha was also very negative towards Krøyer's new wife Marie Triepcke, though the latter's relationship with Krøyer post-dated Krøyer's rejection of Helene Christensen. Krøyer had a big row via an exchange of letters with the Johansens at the beginning of 1891. In Copenhagen on 16 January he wrote to Viggo mentioning a letter he had received from Helene Christensen, and claimed that the Johansens had deliberately taken Christensen into their house in order to exclude Krøyer and his new bride (Loerges 1977: 33).[13] That same month he wrote that 'Mrs Johansen has referred to my wife in a scandalous manner [...] a mouthpiece for the most appalling rumours' (Svanholm 2004: 124-5). Krøyer and his new wife Marie visited Skagen in the summer of 1891 and were accepted by the Anchers and Degn Brøndum, but Martha Johansen didn't visit Skagen again for twenty-five years. The idea of a Utopian society had broken down when human emotions and desires entered the equation. Hence the Johansens are notable absentees from Krøyer's final major painting *St. Hansblus paa Skagens Strand* (*Midsummer's Eve bonfire on Skagen's beach*, 1906; Skagens Museum), as was Helene Christensen, who returned to Denmark from the USA after less than three years but didn't become the church organist in Skagen until 1908 (Svanholm 2006: 62).

The Krøyers' marriage was not a happy one as P. S. Krøyer had mental problems. In 1902 Marie met the Swedish composer Hugo Alfvén in Sicily and they came to Skagen in 1904. Marie had a daughter by him in 1905, forcing P. S. Krøyer to agree to a divorce. Krøyer included the couple in his final masterwork, but detached them from everyone else and painted flames roaring towards them, as if in a form of pagan retribution. Krøyer, of course, could only think of the light in his picture: '[...] it has become too dark – the sky did not have the pale radiance of Midsummer Eve' (Krøyer cited in Svanholm 2006: 206).

In conclusion, Skagen provided a cocoon in the north of Denmark, an isolated and exclusive place where artists had an abundance of source material and motifs for their pictures in terms of both the local populace and the picturesque coastal setting. It can be claimed that a minority of the population of the local fisherfolk were exploited like an indigenous tribe discovered by ambitious anthropologists, or alternatively that they were grateful for the opportunity of a modicum of money and fame provided by elite outsiders. I believe that one needs to take a nuanced view of the artist/fisherfolk relationship and contest that it is not a one-sided view of peasant people exploited for their own ends by uncaring artists. Instead I suggest that there is a degree of symbiosis in this relationship, which is either mutualistic or commensalistic, but not parasitic; each party either gains from the relationship, or at the very least does not suffer from it. What is incontestable is that in Skagen this relationship led to the creation of a significant body of art that precipitates an enduring dialogue for both an academic and a lay audience.

Endnotes

[1] See Lübbren (2001) and Barrett (2010) for a full discussion.

[2] For a discussion of the family relationships between Andersen, the Rørbyes and the Brøndums, see Barrett (2010: 278).

[3] For visual evidence, see Viggo Johansen's *Self-Portrait* of 1875 (location unknown) in Loerges (1977: 44-45).

[4] See Parker and Pollock (1981: 42-44).

[5] Among the artists in Skagen that summer were Christian Krohg (Norway), Frits Thaulow (Norway) and Wilhelm von Gegerfelt (Sweden).

[6] Not to be confused with the Adrian Stokes who visited Skagen. See footnote 9 below.

[7] A Danish exception was the socially-concerned Erik Henningsen, exemplified by *Summum jus, summa injuria. Barnemordet Summum jus, summum injuria. The Murder of a Child* (1886; Hirschsprung Collection, Copenhagen), a vivid portrayal of infanticide at this time.

[8] The most famous example being Diego Velázquez, *Las Meninas* (1656; Museo del Prado, Madrid).

[9] However there were five British visitors: Adrian Stokes (1854-1935) and his Austrian-born wife Marianne in 1886, and the Newlyn-based Thomas Gotch, Caroline Burland Gotch, and Arthur Tanner in 1889, plus others – including the Greek Jean Altamura in 1876 – which suggests that the overall Scandinavian percentage was a little lower than Lübbren's figure.

[10] For example, J. M. W. Turner *Snow Storm - Steam-Boat off a Harbour's Mouth* (1842; Tate Modern, London).

[11] See Jensen (2011: 136), Saabye (2011a: 234), Jacobs (1985: 105) and Cox (2014: 416).

[12] Michael Ancher in *En Barnedaab A Christening* may have been painted by his wife Anna Ancher (Nielsen-Bergqvist 2018: 61).

[13] Helene Christensen can be seen in several of Viggo Johansen's pictures of this period, notably top-right in *Glade Jul Merry Christmas* (1891; Hirschsprung Collection, Copenhagen), and far-right in *Afteninteriør Evening Interior* (1890; location unknown, see Loerges 1977: 80).

References

Barrett, B. D. (2010). *Artists on the Edge: The Rise of Coastal Artists' Colonies, 1880-1920.* Amsterdam: Amsterdam University Press.

Bell, J. (2016), 'Taken from life: The unsettling art of death photography', BBC News, 5 June. https://www.bbc.co.uk/news/uk-england-36389581 (accessed 2 August 2019).

Benjamin, W. (1982 [1934]). 'The Author as Producer' in Frascina, F. and Harrison C. (eds.) *Modern Art and Modernism: A Critical Anthology*, London: Open University, pp. 213-216.

Berman, P. G. (2007). 'Skagen and the Modern Breakthrough' in Berman, P. G. (ed.) *In Another Light: Danish Painting in the Nineteenth Century.* London: Thames and Hudson, pp. 133-177.

Cox, J. D. (2014). *The Impact of Nordic Art in Europe 1878-1889.* White Rose online e-thesis, University of Leeds: http://etheses.whiterose.ac.uk/10406/

Fjågesund, P. and Symes, R. (2003). *The Northern Utopia: British Perceptions of Norway in the Nineteenth Century.* Amsterdam: Editions Rodopi B.V.

Jacobs, M. (1985). *The Good and Simple Life: Artist Colonies in Europe and America.* Oxford: Phaidon.

Jensen, M. B. (2005). 'Dem og os: Forholdet mellem fiskerne og kunstnerne' in Jensen, M. B. (ed.), *At male sit privatliv: Skagensmalernes selviscenesættelse.* Skagen: Skagens Museum, pp. 106-151.

Jensen, M. B. (2011). *Brøndums Dining Room – In Gratitude for Happy Days*, Skagen: Skagens Museum.

Krohg, C. and Garrett, P. R. (2017 [1894]). 'Skagen 1894', *Art in Translation*, 9 (2), pp. 210-218.

Loerges, M. (1977). *I Medgang og Modgang: Portræt af kunstneren Viggo Johansens hustru Martha Johansen.* Copenhagen: Hernov.

Lübbren, N. (2001). *Rural Artists' Colonies in Europe: 1870-1910.* New Brunswick and New Jersey: Rutgers University Press.

Monrad, K. and Hornung, P. M. (2002). *The Modern Breakthrough in Danish Painting 1870-1890*. Copenhagen: Golden Days in Copenhagen.

More, T. (1978 [1516]). 'The Second Book of Utopia', in More, T. (ed.), *Utopia*. London: Dent, pp. 55-135.

Mullins, E. (1967). *Alfred Wallis: Cornish Primitive Painter*. London: Macdonald.

Nielsen-Bergqvist, J. (2018). 'A Christening, a Monument' in Vejlby, A. S. (ed.) *Michael Ancher and the Women of Skagen*, Skagen, Copenhagen and Ribe: Skagens Museum, The Hirschsprung Collection, Ribe Kunstmuseum, pp. 36-67.

O'Neill, M. (2014). *Cornwall's 'Fisherfolk': Art and Artifice*. Bristol: Sansom & Co.

Parker, R. and Pollock, G. (1981). *Old Mistresses: women, art and ideology*, London: Routledge & Kegan Paul, pp. 42-44.

Saabye, M. (1990). *P. S. Krøyer's Fotografier*. Copenhagen: The Hirschsprung Collection.

Saabye, M. (2011a). *Krøyer: An International Perspective*. Copenhagen and Skagen: The Hirschsprung Collection and Skagens Museum.

Saabye, M. (2011b). *100 Years of Danish Art*. Copenhagen: The Hirschsprung Collection.

Svanholm, L. (2004 [2001]). *Northern Light: The Skagen Painters*. Copenhagen: Gyldendal.

Svanholm, L. (2006). *Damerne på Skagen*. Copenhagen: Gyldendal.

A Swedish Landscape? Nature and Identity in the Painting of Gustaf Fjæstad and Helmer Osslund

Isabelle Gapp

'No, Sweden was not the land for art' (Bergh, cited in Facos 2001: 207). Such was the proclamation made by the Swedish painter Richard Bergh who, along with Carl Larsson and Nils Kreuger, among others, had rebuked the old-fashioned traditions of the Royal Academy of Art in Stockholm, and instead imposed upon themselves self-exile in Paris, 'att lämna "barbarlandet" Sverige för att bli kosmopoliter' (Lagerlöf 2015: 38) (leaving 'barbaric' Sweden to become cosmopolitans). For Nordic artists of the 1880s the styles of impressionism and realism could only be studied and mastered in France; there was no desire to remain at home. However, the allure of Paris soon wore off. Artists of this first generation of 'National Romantic' painters, as they were later characterised, soon realised the importance of painting their native home as opposed to mimicking their French surroundings. Yet for Gustaf Fjæstad (1868-1948), who received no Parisian training, and Helmer Osslund (1866-1938), who first travelled to Paris in 1894, the influence of those artistic trends emerging from France is open to exaggeration.[1] Moving beyond the Symbolism of the 1890s, as identified in the work of their predecessors, the work of Osslund and Fjæstad highlights a reliance on the qualities of their surrounding environment, as observed through a concentrated application of colour and technique. As a result, the decorative winter scenes of Fjæstad and the richly coloured landscapes of Osslund, when viewed in tandem, reveal the diversity of the Swedish landscape and contribute to a more expansive idea of north. This comparative study, moreover, lends insight into what 'national identity' and 'home' looked like in painting after Symbolism.

The term 'National Romanticism' is often used to identify the Symbolist artists working in Scandinavia during the 1890s; those who sought to depict their native landscape, culture and heritage, and to instil in the viewer a personal and emotive response through their compositions (see Facos 1998). The exhibition, *Northern Light: Realism and Symbolism in Scandinavian Painting, 1880-1910*, which was the first collective exhibition on Scandinavian art in over sixty years when it was staged in 1982, thus established an 'ism' in which the period of 1880-90s Nordic painting could be situated. Curated by the late art historian Kirk Varnedoe, and his then students Michelle Facos and Patricia Berman, this was not merely a display of art created in the same period; it was an attempt to collate these artists together. Seen as following in the symbolist style, a description sparsely used in the late nineteenth century,[2] with France as their main source of inspiration, a more localised model for categorising these artists was required. As such, the concept of 'National Romanticism' came to be. Defined as a variant of continental symbolism, it was a term which referred to Nordic art of the 1890s.[3]

Landscape painting gained unprecedented prominence during this period; it became a way to localise and visualise a national identity. Bergh discussed the role of nature and 'believed that Nordic art was independent because it sprang from an affinity with the native landscape' (Varnedoe 1988: 50). The personal emotive response of the artist was intrinsic to understanding the landscape in their work: that first the artist must paint what he or she feels before providing a representation of the land. In the case of Osslund, however, he often placed emphasis first on the landscape before him, and subsequently imbued it with the sentiment of the artist. Roald Nasgaard reiterates this sentiment in his 1984 exhibition catalogue for *The Mystic North*, where he quoted Osslund as having remarked that a work of art 'must first of all be based on the study of nature and not be a pure creation of the imagination' (Nasgaard 1984: 88).

The affinity between mankind and nature, specifically in the works of Fjæstad and Osslund, emerges through their artistic dependency on the landscape. The lakes and mountains extending across the country not only provided an abundance of motifs which sustained their artistic lifestyles, but also identified their homes. For Osslund it was the allure of the rolling hills of his native Norrland, where he spent much of his early life; Fjæstad, by contrast, born to Norwegian parents, and raised in Stockholm following the untimely death of his father, was seeking a landscape which not only inspired him but where he could also create a home. The first home Gustaf and his wife Maja had in Värmland was, to the painter's disappointment, not his own but rather through economic necessity rented from artist Christian Eriksson and his wife Jeanne Tramcourt. Despite the unplanned start to their new lives, as his daughter Agnetha later wrote, 'Gustaf skulle äntligen inse att Värmland var hemma' (Fjæstad 1981: 53) (Gustaf would eventually realise that Värmland was home). Fjæstad remained in Värmland until his death in 1948.

Whereas Osslund 'recorded the raw beauty of the Swedish wilderness during the colourful transitional seasons', Fjæstad 'specialised in snow scenes' (Facos 1998: 147); a distinction which marks the prevalence of seasonal change in the artists' individual oeuvres. An example of such can be found in the infinitesimal detail of Fjæstad's painting *Rimfrost på is* (*Hoar Frost on Ice*, Fig. 1). Here, the emphasis is on the flakes of encrusted snow which have settled upon the surface of the frozen lake; a blanket of newly-fallen snow encircling the composition. In much of his work Fjæstad abstained from the wide perspective; instead he painted close-up, magnifying the patterns and details which could be found in the landscape, all the while observing this through a

Isabelle Gapp

Fig. 1: *Gustaf Fjæstad:* Rimfrost på is (Hoar Frost on Ice), *1901. Oil on canvas. 150 x 200 cm. Photo: Tord Lund/Thielska Galleriet. Reproduced with permission of Thielska Galleriet.*

colour scheme, which in contrast to Osslund was 'restricted to whites, greys, and earth browns' revealing 'Fjæstad's feeling for the nuances of neutral colour tonalities' (Nasgaard 1984: 78). This particular attachment to the wooded winter landscape came about following Fjæstad's move to Värmland, specifically the area surrounding Lake Racken. The gentler topography of this area, unlike the rugged wilderness against a mountainous backdrop as in the neighbouring provinces of Jämtland and Härjedalen, provided Fjæstad with the inspiration he sought (although he would find this inspiration to be at its most fruitful during the winter months). Furthermore, as a one-time world champion speed-skater for one English mile (Fjæstad 1981: 21), it is not surprising that Fjæstad was instinctively drawn towards the frozen landscape. His paintings, moreover, evoke the various types of snow that come about during the winter period, from the *Skarsnö* (snow crust) of *Från Dovrefjäll* (*From Dovrefjäll*, 1904; Thielska Gallery, Stockholm) where the snow has frozen after a slight thaw, to the *Rimfrost* (rime ice) of his painting *Hoar Frost on Ice* where patterns of ice have formed upon the surface.

At the time when Fjæstad was working, scenes of winter were rare in Swedish painting, but it soon became a popular motif – perceived as being inherently Nordic – with artists including Finnish painters Akseli Gallen-Kallela (1865-1931) and Pekka Halonen (1865-1933) exploring the similar effects of snow on the landscape. It also ties in with the growing prestige of the Arctic which captivated the minds of writers, artists, and most importantly, explorers. The understanding of Scandinavia as a landscape submerged in cold and darkness, where the 'Scandinavian countries are cold countries [...] icebound and snow-covered, overspread by a leaden sky' (Townsend 1912: 2), is refuted by Fjæstad's paintings which combine stylisation with realistic definition; where nature is not bleak, but beautiful. Facos considers the 'ornamental complexity' (Facos 1998: 187) in Fjæstad's approach to nature, and as such, how he follows 'the National Romantic dictum to paint subjects about which one feels most passionate' (Facos 1998: 187). A similar passion for the subject is also found in the works of Osslund, particularly his autumnal scenes. The legacy of 'National Romanticism' and the division of artists by generation perhaps provides a better framework with which to analyse these painters individually; however, it separates the continuity of theme and subject matter which continued to permeate the work of Swedish painters in particular. It furthermore promotes the continued idea of a Symbolist agenda within their works, although what evidence there is to support this is conjectured. The landscape had become self-contained, it no longer relied on a symbolic meaning to be understood. It was nature for nature's sake; and as such became much more representative of what could be deemed typically Swedish.

The prevalence of winter in Fjæstad's oeuvre is contrasted by the overwhelming presence of autumn in the paintings of Osslund. Scenes of winter are rarely found in Osslund's work, although his *Islossning, Faxälven* (*The Ice Breaks Up, Faxälven, c. 1918*; National Museum, Stockholm) provides a rare example, depicting the fracturing ice breaking away from the snow-covered banks of the river, beginning to move once again with the current. Parallel representations of summer were equally uncommon. In 1971 the National Museum in Stockholm staged an exhibition on Osslund, for which a family friend and critic Helge Dahlstedt wrote for the catalogue, drawing upon notes dated 1956, that, 'när han nån gång målade sommaren, gjorde han den gärna dramatisk med dekorativa tunga moln eller med en regnby' (Dahlstedt 1971: 13) ('when he did paint summer, he would instead make it dramatic with heavy, decorative clouds or a rainbow', translation by the author). Instead, it was the colours of autumn which most captivated the artist. Osslund devoted himself to the portrayal of Västernorrland, mainly the areas of Ljungan, Ångermanälven, Faxälven and Indalsälven, before journeying further north into Lappland in 1905 – two regions of the country that were hitherto virtually unexplored in art. The remote regions of the north of Sweden, slowly receding into the Arctic Circle, became synonymous with the painting of Osslund, who after spending time in both America and at great length on the European continent, found in the area surrounding his childhood home the artistic inspiration he had been searching for.

The dramatic and rich effects of autumn on the landscape — 'clear colour, sharply silhouetted forms, and [the] mighty rhythm of seemingly illimitable stretches of mountain and sky' (Brinton 1916: 142) — are what occupy much of Osslund's work. Many of his paintings synthesised the characteristics of this

Fig. 2: *Helmer Osslund:* Hösten (Autumn), *c. 1907. Oil on canvas. 116 x 202 cm. Nationalmuseum, Stockholm. Photo: Hans Thorwid/Nationalmuseum. Copyright: Public domain.*

season, capturing, often in sketch form, the blustery winds and vivid colours of the changing leaves and tempestuous waters, frequently painted in the landscape surrounding his birth town of Sundsvall. A much more refined and tamed example of Osslund's landscapes is found in *Hösten* (*Autumn*, c. 1907; Fig. 2), which was one of four paintings depicting the seasons created for the home of leather industry owner Emil A. Matton in Gävle. This work highlights a decorative quality akin to that found in Fjæstad's painting, moving away from the unruly handling of colour and paint as found in Osslund's sketches.

The noted decorative quality in both Osslund's and Fjæstad's work has been tied to *Japonisme*, and yet there is little to no scholarship to suggest that either artist was directly influenced by Japanese painting. Rather it is more likely that these painters would have experienced the art of Japan through a proliferation of Japanese prints within Swedish art circles. Although the Danish painter Karl Madsen had published his influential volume *Japansk Malerkunst (Japanese Painting)* in 1885, stylistic assumptions cannot be drawn between Madsen's writing and Fjæstad and Osslund's work. Recent exhibitions on the subject, however, have sought to highlight the Nordic-Japanese artistic synergies that arguably existed during the late nineteenth and early twentieth century.[4] Beyond this, I would endeavour to propose a stronger affinity between Fjæstad and the Arts & Crafts movement spearheaded by William Morris. This is not only exemplified in his paintings, but also in his tapestries and furniture design. Beyond the influence of the Arts & Crafts and *Japonisme*, it is also important to consider the role of nature as a facilitator of this design – that although the rhythmic application of paint might denote an underlying stylistic influence, it only adds to the already patterned surface of the landscape.

The natural decorativeness of the landscape can best be found in Osslund's sketches. He would create these images upon sheets of baking paper, pinning them to pieces of cardboard which he used as an easel. He spent days exploring the surrounding landscape, often painting in the early evening as the sun began to set, the twilight hours saturating the colour palette, before returning to his lodging and pinning up that day's paintings to the walls to allow them to dry. Osslund placed great emphasis on exploring the landscape himself, and, as a result, very few of his works are large scale finished canvases (as these required a studio to be completed). By consistently immersing himself in this environment, even into old age when arthritis riddled his hands, he created some of the most identifiable paintings of the northern Swedish landscape. His autumnal paintings were best described by Dahlstedt:

Osslund har målat natur i Norrland under alla årstider. Mest älskade han hösten med dess glödande färger, som i Norrland och fjällen brinner klarare och intensivare än söderut, när frosten med ens biter i löven på träd och buskar, i riset och gräset på marken och hastigt färgar om grönskan, innan den hunnit vissna och mögla. (Dahlstedt 1971: 12).

(Osslund has painted the nature of Norrland throughout all the seasons. He loved autumn the most, with its glowing colours, which in Norrland and in the fells of Lapland burn clearer and more intensely than in the south; where the frost bites the leaves of the trees and the bushes, on the twigs and grass on the ground and quickly colours in the surrounding foliage, before it has managed to wither and rot.)

The vitality of the colours used and the impasto texture of the paint have often been perceived as reflecting the training Osslund received in Paris with an emphasis on synthetism. In citing an article from the *Svensk Konstkröniker* written in 1905, Nasgaard proceeds to support the hypothesis that the work of both Fjæstad and Osslund brought with it a 'fresher more brutal view of nature than the painters of the 1890s, less mood, less synthetism, less symbolism' (Nasgaard 1984: 85). However, Facos remarks that 'the lessons of Synthetism emerge here in the streamlined contours and broad areas of colour, which Osslund used to create a static, recognisably Nordic landscape' (Facos 1998: 163). With regard to Fjæstad, Facos argues that he used 'Synthetist strategies for a decorative and emotional impact' (Facos 1998: 187); and similarly, Torsten Gunnarsson wrote that alongside Osslund and Kreuger, 'all three turned to a form of Synthetism' (Gunnarsson 1998: 247). This synthetist approach was something Osslund learned during his time in Paris, where he studied under proponents of the movement, namely Paul Gauguin and the Danish painter J. F. Willumsen. It was a style which placed emphasis on the combination of artistic feeling with an aestheticism of style, technique, and colour.[5] Although there is a sense of this in Osslund's works, they do not endeavour to epitomise a style; rather they convey the artist's own environmental reality. At no point during the artist's career in Sweden does he purposefully associate his work with the synthetist movement. Rather, the association with this term, by Nasgaard, Facos and Gunnarsson, considers him as a Nordic parallel to mainstream continental trends.

Both Osslund and Fjæstad's work became emblematic of a Swedish landscape hitherto unexplored. In so doing, their work represents a burgeoning national idiom; one less preoccupied with France and continental Europe, and instead focused on the landscape of home. However, that said, a sense of national pride in the landscape did not remain exclusively theirs. The sphere of influence of the works of Osslund and Fjæstad traversed geographical boundaries and extended across the landscape of the northern hemisphere. It contributes to a greater understanding of the 'north', of the relationship between art and culture, and a desire to explore the landscape both near and far. In 1912-1913 the works of Fjæstad were exhibited in the touring *Exhibition of Contemporary Scandinavian Art* that opened in New York in December 1912. Here, they were met with high regard, with the critic Elizabeth Luther Cary writing for the magazine *Art & Progress* that he was 'remarkable in his interpretation of snow,' using 'canvases of vast size' but 'filling them with the sentiment of his subject' (Cary 1913: 857). Meanwhile, it was with the *Pan-Pacific Exposition* of 1915, and subsequent *Exhibition of Swedish Painting* in 1916, that Osslund's work was first introduced to a North American audience. Among those influenced by the work of the aforementioned artists were the Canadian Group of Seven. Formed as a group in 1920, these painters had long sought 'to throw off the alien influences of art movements long since discarded in Europe' (Davies 1932: 16), notably the Barbizon school, and find a more accurate, and preferably non-European, way to represent the Canadian landscape. However, one of the founding members, J. E. H. MacDonald, later recalled in a lecture given in 1931 and published in the *Northward Journal* in 1980 that there was an 'an affinity of inspiration' (MacDonald 1980: 10) between their idea of art and that of Scandinavia, and that 'except in minor points, the pictures might all have been Canadian' (MacDonald, cited in Hill 1996: 48). This transference of one artist's idea of home had resonated with another group; that the visual identity of one nation had helped another group of artists find a way to embody the vast wilderness and changing seasons of their own home.[6]

The visualisation of the landscape as a way of establishing a national identity is something which occurs throughout the Nordic nations – as highlighted in this chapter in both Swedish and Finnish examples. The attachment to the land was something which was inherently personal, and, as such, was the means through which a study of nationality, regionality and individuality could be made. With the work of Fjæstad and Osslund, although only two examples in a much wider sphere of Nordic landscape painters, the seasonal representation of nature and the land which they inhabited helped form an idea of what 'naturally' represented their nation, discarding urbanisation and instead pushing back to the far-flung corners of the country. These painters further contributed to the necessary study required to move Nordic art history beyond a national idiom. More than thirty years on from Varnedoe's *Northern Light*, a broader understanding is required. To properly understand and place Swedish and Nordic art in a wider European and Northern Circumpolar context, it is not enough to look at this period of art history solely as a contributor to nation-building, but rather to allow for an extension of current thinking which goes beyond the strict confines of 'National Romanticism'. Examining the artistic exchange between the Nordic nations and North America finally allows some room for manoeuvre. By not merely adhering to a study of 'isms' the opportunities are endless.

Endnotes

All translations from Swedish are by the author of this chapter, unless otherwise indicated.

[1] For further information on the vitae of Gustaf Fjæstad and Helmer Osslund, see Fjæstad (1981) and Palmgren & Granberg (1937).

[2] The term Symbolism was rarely used by Swedish artists. However, in a letter to the artist Georg Pauli in 1893, Bergh wrote regarding his painting *Vision: Motiv från Visby* (1894; National Museum, Stockholm): 'one immediately found Symbolist suggestion – a cloud was no longer merely a cloud but assumed a double meaning' (Facos 1998: 132).

[3] A similar phrasing of the term 'romantic nationalism' can also be found with reference to Norwegian painting of the period between 1840 and 1870, with 'Neo-Romanticism' used to denote those Norwegian painters working from the late 1880s onwards.

[4] For more on the relationship between Nordic and Japanese art see recent exhibitions: *Japanomania in the Nordic Countries 1875-1918*, curated by Gabriel P. Weisberg in 2016; *När Japan kom till Värmland. Japonism hos Rackstadkonstnärerna 1880-1920*, held at Thielska Gallery, Stockholm, 17 February-3 June 2018; and *Mellan Björk och Bambu: Japansk inspiration i Sundborn – nu och då*, at Carl Larsson Gården in Sundborn, 17 June-19 August 2018.

[5] Synthetism emerged in France in 1888 and was first seen by Richard Bergh and Prince Eugen in Paris in 1889, where they witnessed an exhibition at Café Volpini staged by Paul Gauguin, Emile Bernard and their Pont-Aven colleagues. In addition, two exhibitions staged in Copenhagen in 1892 and 1893, featuring works by Gauguin and Vincent van Gogh, are likely to have been seen by a larger contingent of Nordic artists. The style of synthetism sought to distil the natural world into simple shapes and pigments. For further information on Nordic art and synthetism see Facos (1998) and Gunnarsson (1998).

[6] Further discussion pertaining to the relationship between the Group of Seven and Scandinavia can be found in Nasgaard (1984) and more recently in Ohlsen (2011).

References

Brinton, C. (1916). *Impressions of the Art at the Panama-Pacific Exposition.* New York: John Lane Company.

Cary, E.L. (1913). 'Scandinavian Art.' *Art and Progress*, 4, pp. 851-857.

Dahlstedt, H. (1971). 'Helmer Osslund, utdrag ur minnesanteckningar 1956', in Reuterswärd, P. (ed.), *Helmer Osslund – Norrlands målare*. Stockholm: AB Egnellska Boktryckeriet, pp. 11-13.

Davies, B. (1932). 'The Canadian Group of Seven', *The American Magazine of Art*, 25, July, pp. 13-22.

Facos, M. (1998). *Nationalism and the Nordic Imagination: Swedish Art of the 1890s.* Berkeley: University of California Press.

Facos, M. (2001). 'Primitivism in Sweden: Dormant Desire or Fictional Identity', in Jessup, L. (ed.), *Antimodernism and Artistic Experience: Policing the Boundaries of Modernity.* Toronto: University of Toronto Press, pp. 206-215.

Fjæstad, A. (1981). *Gustaf och Maja Fjæstad: Ett konstnärspar.* Karlstad: NWT:s Förlag.

Gunnarsson, T. (1998). *Nordic Landscape Painting in the Nineteenth Century.* New Haven and London: Yale University Press.

Hill, C. C. (1996). *The Group of Seven: Art for a Nation.* Michigan: McClelland & Stewart Inc.

Lagerlöf, M. R. (2015). 'Saga, Myt & Det Narrativa', in Meister, A., Prytz, D. and Sidén, K. (eds.). *Symbolism och Dekadens.* Stockholm: Prins Eugens Waldemarsudde, Stockholm, pp. 17-55.

MacDonald, J. E. H. (1980). 'Scandinavian Art', *Northward Journal*, 18-19, pp. 9-35.

Nasgaard, R. (1984). *The Mystic North: Symbolist Landscape Painting in Northern Europe and North America 1890-1940.* Toronto: University of Toronto Press.

Ohlsen, N. (2011). '"This is what we want to do with Canada" – Reflections of Scandinavian Landscape Painting in the Work of

Tom Thomson and the Group of Seven', in Dejardin, I. A. C. and Concannon, A. (eds.), *Painting Canada: Tom Thomson and the Group of Seven*. London: Philip Wilson Publishers, pp. 47-54.

Palmgren, N. and Granberg, H. (1937). *Helmer Osslund - Norrlands målare*. Stockholm: AB Svensk Litteratur.

Townsend, J. (1912). 'The Scandinavian Pictures', *American Art News*, 11 (12), p. 2.

Varnedoe, K. (1988). *Northern Light: Nordic Art at the Turn of the Century*. New Haven and London: Yale University Press.

PRESENT HOMES

Nordic Sound Art: Aspects of an Artistic Collectivity

Aya Shimano-Bardai

Introduction

'Sound art' is a polysemous term referring to a multifaceted and composite genre. As a result of its historical connection to music and visual arts, and the multiplicity and hybridity of its forms, the genre is open to various definitions and thus raises many debates and discussions. Since the emergence of sound art in the 1950s and throughout its development, Nordic artists have engaged in opening a considerable number of galleries, collectives, festivals and exhibitions which are associated as much with the music as with the artistic field. With the aim of exploring new ways of experimenting and questioning former methods, the artists within this genre have been actively participating in broadening the field of definition, interpretation and creation.

The growing density of projects, events and locations dedicated to sound art in the Nordic countries reveals the strong participation of communities in taking the initiative to develop this art form. This is one indication of the research potential of this topic within the broad field of sound in the arts. Furthermore, many of these initiatives and projects set out with the ambition of developing sound art in a collective spirit within the Nordic countries, pointing towards the construction of a certain artistic identity in this specific geographical context.

How might we define and shape this collective approach to the study of sound art? How can we transcend the respective ambiguities of, on the one hand, this art form without a fixed definition, and, on the other hand, the concept of the North? Looking at the artistic and curatorial aspects of few contemporary Nordic sound art projects, this chapter questions the influence of the geographical factor on artistic outcomes and its contribution to the study of stylistic relations.

Historical background

Due to its attachment to music and visual arts, as well as the multiplicity of its forms, sound art is still an under-theorised practice. The first use of the term itself appears in the 1980s, often attributed to the composer Dan Lander (Licht 2007: 11), though its history started earlier. From the mid-twentieth century, music and arts reached a turning point: the field was opened for an aesthetic approach to sound. With the continuous evolution of technological tools, sound experiments ceaselessly developed within the interdisciplinary works of composers, visual artists and curators, integrating sound in exhibition spaces that had once been silent. Listening culture expanded outside of its conventional structures, making way for new modes of writing and listening to music and sound.

Sound art finds its origins at different points in history, particularly with the influence of the early noise experiments of the Italian futurists, the linguistic approach in the sound compositions of Dadaists and Lettrists, the works of Fluxus artists and kinetic art. John Cage's experimental music and La Monte Young's continuous sound works were also major contributors to this merging of fields. Sound art was thus founded with the works of notable sound artists and composers such as Max Neuhaus (*Listen,* 1966; *Times Square,* 1977), Maryanne Amacher (*City links,* 1967), Alvin Lucier (*I am sitting in a room,* 1969) and Christina Kubisch (*Electrical walks,* 1970). These represented the emergence of new sonic forms, introducing the first site-specific sound installations, sound walks and the continuous expansion of sonic performances outside of concert halls.

Along with the emergence of new fields and terms in that period, sound-based practices were being reconsidered, especially in terms of their integration into different art spaces. Often used as a general term for works that focus on sound, sound art is variously explained as an expanded concept of sculpture (Schulz 2002: 14) or a category of installation art that involves working with spaces both acoustically and sculpturally (Metzger 2006: 53). It is also defined as sound combined with visual practices, organised in a manner that differentiates it from more traditional practices associated with music (Toop 1999: 107). Sound art's rich historical background and forms still make it complex to get a hold of a fixed definition, consequently extending the framework of its studies and practices.

Developments in the Nordic countries

The scope of Nordic music and art also underwent similar changes during the same period. In parallel with the development of visual arts, the Elektronmusik Studion (EMS) opened in Stockholm during the early 1960s and produced influential works and musical collaborations at that time. Fylkingen, which had been founded in 1933 in Stockholm as a chamber music association, was reoriented towards experimental music to pioneer text-sound composition. This had a major impact on the evolution of contemporary music in Sweden, experimenting with vocal expression and communication through language. In parallel, Norway experienced the electroacoustic music of Arne Nordheim who founded the Norsk Studio for Elektronisk Musikk in 1975. After that studio was dissolved, the Norwegian Network for Technology, Acoustics and Music (NOTAM) was established in 1993, sustaining the development of electronic music activities. In 1986, the Danish Institute of Electroacoustic Music was founded in Aarhus, Denmark, also the homeland of the pioneering female electronic composer, Else Marie Pade. In addition to electronic and electroacoustic music, the powerful emergence of noise and experimental music also had a major impact on the development of sound art. Some of its figures such as Lasse Marhaug, Tore Honoré Bøe, John Hegre and Maja Ratkje show the implication of noise music in diverse interdisciplinary approaches.

In order to create homes for these new sonic experiments, many spaces continued to be built and organised in the Nordic countries. Examples include the Creative Room for Art and Computing in Stockholm, Atelier Nord in Oslo, I/o/lab in Stavanger and the Bergen Center for Electronic Arts in Bergen. Lydgalleriet, a sound art gallery founded in 2007 in Bergen, made the city an important spot for Nordic sonic artists and collectives. An active environment is also found in Helsinki with MUU, an interdisciplinary art collective founded in 1987. MUU organises projects presenting various forms of experimental arts, as well as the *MUU for Ears* series of publications and events on Nordic and international sound art. Petri Kuljuntausta later opened Akusmata in 2011, a sound art gallery which often collaborates with MUU, a space for media art, video and performances with sound as central subject.

Consequently, an important number of festivals dedicated to sonic practices started opening from 2000, such as the Nordic sound art festival LAK and avant-garde music festival Klang in Copenhagen, the contemporary art, science and technology festival Click in Helsingør and the contemporary art and sound art festival SPOR in Aarhus. In Bergen, Borealis and EKKO festivals annually take over many venues in the city. Skálar in Seyðisfjörður and Sequences in Reykjavík also extended and integrated new sonic forms into the contemporary spectrum. These festivals explore sound art in its intersections with visual and performance arts, conceiving the events within different frameworks, ranging from installation, fixed-media, interactive to site-specific works, and diffusion techniques developed within different curated, public and urban environments. Though often associated with experimental, new media art or electronic music, sound art has gained prominence in hybrid venues and spaces.

Collective projects

In the wake of the first sonic experiments and their development in contemporary milieux, the aim of putting a 'Nordic practice' forward in different collective sound art projects crystallised. This aim is evinced by the numerous projects and collective initiatives regrouping and uniting practitioners of Scandinavia and neighbouring countries. LARM, founded in 2004 after the launch of the Nordic Sound Art Festival, was a female Nordic sound artist collective. The three criteria – female, Nordic, and sound practice – constitute the fundamental structure of LARM, putting a focus on gender in parallel with practices elaborated within the regional territory. For a few years, LARM contributed to promoting both sound art produced in the Nordic countries and the strong involvement of female artists in the field through exhibitions, festivals and lectures. Sachiko Hayashi, curator of the Fylkingen Hz Net Gallery, explains how the participation of many artists made the festival international despite its Nordic criterion, and how it provided a more adequate reflection of the present day 'Nordic' (Hayashi 2007: 37). From Hayashi's viewpoint, the Nordic criterion in the LARM project is considered to be inclusive, hinting that it is a matter of a collective work that builds strong links around the same artistic medium. A brief look at the regrouped keywords, categories and terms chosen by the artists to reflect their works already reveals diversity and an interdisciplinary approach,[1] with a wide spectrum of objects, techniques, influences, diffusion and reception modes.

In the academic context, the Nordic Sound Art Programme, launched in 2007, set out specific geographical criteria for the participants, creating a cross-Nordic study programme for art students. In fact, an overview of the programme's presentation, description and content clearly shows how it covered a variety of sonic productions, concepts and methods. While marking out the localities where sound art was made was one of its defining elements, an aim of the programme was to cover a broad range of knowledge in audio-technologies and theoretical introductions, working with sound particularly in relation to visual arts (Søchting and Kulberg 2009: 9). Thus, in different creative contexts, the artistic aims and resulting works of both LARM and Nordic Sound Art Programme were equally focused on diversifying artistic outcomes. With the situational context as the leading factor that underpinned the chosen title and criteria, they strongly highlighted an interdisciplinary approach in their works, with an accent on approaching the sonic dimension in relation to visual arts. With the use of different creative methods, forms varied from installation, sculpture, performance, radiophonic and video works.

Even if various techniques are put into practice, field recording has been important in reaching and using specific sound locations. Sounds captured in the Nordic regions have been considered for their qualities as a material and as an extensive object of study in many sound works, such as the compositions in the *Sleppet* exhibition.[2] Presented in Bergen in 2007, these were created following a trip in western Norway during spring thaw. Inviting the artists Steve Roden, Chris Watson, Marc Behrens, Natasha Barrett, Jana Winderen and Bjarne Kvinnsland, the point of departure of this project was Edvard Grieg's interest in sounds he discovered in Norwegian nature. Sound materials were specifically captured on location between Sandane, Jostedalsbreen and Utvær, making field recording the direct tool to create acousmatic microcosms: the nature and rural acoustics of western Norway were the elementary sources. Regarding technology as a tool and Norwegian nature as a subject, Jørgen

Larsson, curator of the *Sleppet* exhibition, emphasises how both visual and acoustic landscapes in the North need protection, given their rarity and importance in acoustic ecology or broader sound art productions (Larsson 2009: 28).

Exploring and representing Nordic regions through sound is undertaken by many works and projects, rendering the northern soundscape itself a central focus in sound art. Regardless of the final shape these sounds take, in their figurative or narrative forms, the importance of the Northern soundscape is indicated by the act of making these field recordings in the presented locations and a common interest in seeking peculiar sound sources. These aspects were explored in the field recordings conducted for the sound portraits of Göteborg in *The Hidden City* (2004) accompanying the work of writer Magnus Haglund and photographer Stefan Schneider, which explores aspects of the cultural and political scope of the city from 1850. Similarly, the installation *Norway Remixed* (2002) presented at the Oslo central railway station gathered the works of artists in which sounds were captured from different parts of Norway. Produced by the Norwegian Broadcasting Corporation and NOTAM, the curatorial idea was to bring the whole country together through sound, inviting the public to reflect on life around the country and what the inhabitants have in common (Rudi 2003: 151).

Some solo works have also addressed the representation of the North through sound. On a larger geographical scale, artist Susan Philipsz uses sound transmissions in *The Distant Sound* (2014), an artwork that represents the cultural connections between Denmark, Sweden and Norway. Through the Grimeton radio station in Sweden from which the piece was first broadcast, Philipsz's piece explores Scandinavian coastlines, cultural history and landscapes through the theme of 'distance'.[3] The final installation combines sound, photography and film that reflect water as a common link between these countries.

Given the extent of these collective projects and initiatives, it should be possible to assess whether or not Nordic sound art represents the emergence of a specific practice. In this regard, the curatorial approach behind the collective exhibition *The Idea of North* introduces an interesting line of thought. In reference to the experimental radio documentary with the same title produced by pianist Glenn Gould,[4] the exhibition invited artists from the Nordic countries to present sound based works that questioned the concept of North. Presented in Canada, Norway and Iceland, the curatorial idea underpinning this exhibition was to redefine the North as more than a geographic position, exploring the concept and cultural mythology of 'North' as a metaphor for the unknown possibilities of both site and sound. Curator Rhonda Corvese emphasises the fact that people have perceptions of the North which are not only related to geography or weather, but which are also psychological. She gives the example of how some people consider travelling North as a journey into unknown possibilities (Corvese 2006: 13). She adds that for her, there is an aspect of the unknown, of a frontier and an experimentation in both sound and the North, concluding with a discussion of how defining sound is as hard as defining the North (Corvese 2006: 13). In other words, we are still exploring sound and we are still exploring the North.

Curatorial initiatives to promote Nordic sound art have expanded outside of this region. The *Horizonic* exhibition in 2012 invited artists from Greenland, Iceland, the Faroe Islands, Svalbard and Northern Norway, and was partly presented in Paris. The invited artists worked around the curatorial reflection formulated through these questions: 'What does the High North sound like? What particular qualities does this far horizon with its great spaces impart to the sense of hearing, to sound, to silence?' (Ásdís Ólafsdóttir and Eudes 2012: 6). The 'High North' seemingly refers to a far distant region, an image projected in recordings of Norwegian seagulls, portraits reflecting the winter in Svalbard and references to historic Greenland through installations and performances.

But then, are we falling into the symbolic trap related to climate, nature, the unknown and faraway? Is an imaginary of the North built through sonic practices? The concept of Borealism — the discourse of the South about the North[5] — seems to be as present in sound art as in other fields of study. If nature is considered one of the paradigms of the imaginary North, it is not only a matter of the visible but also of the audible nature. In their figurative or narrative forms, works conducted in and from these presented locations and the common interest in seeking peculiar sound sources show the importance of the Northern soundscape. The physical distance shifts the discourse to a different angle; imagery-oriented elements are thus taking a central focus, reflecting on an aspect of 'fascination' before the Nordic soundscape.

Concluding thoughts

Considering the plethora of sonic possibilities on conceptual, phenomenological and philosophical levels, it would not be relevant to identify sound art practices only though peculiar characteristics of image and sound locations. In fact, these aspects are not exclusively applied in the definition of a 'Nordic sound art', but rather exist as possibilities that expand our understanding of sound and its consideration on a wider scale. As a subject or as a creative source, we can stress that some of the strong features of Nordic sound art rely on Nordic landscape and soundscape specificities, collaborative approaches, creative diversity and an encouragement of sound-based practices in their intersection with visual arts. As some artists and audience seem to be responsive to approaching sound through this idea of North, a curatorial approach also plays an important role in building a cultural understanding of these regions through sonic works.

Thus, if the concepts of imaginary and cold are strongly evoked in other fields such as literature or film, there is coherence in applying and questioning Borealism in sound art as well. Through sonic works, this discourse could offer insights into the perception and representation of the North. However, the interchangeability of all the aspects of sound art practice, as discussed in this chapter, invites us to interrogate creative methods. In other words, the subject of Nordic sound art is not solely a matter of this region's representation. Sound is both a material form enhancing other visual elements and a prominent subject which marks specific cultural, geographical or historical connections.

We could assume that the prevailing emphasis in Nordic sound art on geographical specificity is due to cultural policy, or even to strategic promotion of a trend. Since a good deal of Nordic sound art hinges on cultural stereotypes, these questions cannot be overlooked. Yet, also in evidence is the ambition to expand the practice of sound art by defining it, not least by situating it specifically in the geographical context in which it is evolving. Nordic sound art is thus not only a projection of what we assume North is, or a version of what practitioners themselves project, but is also a contribution to integrating sound art into the field of contemporary arts as a full-blown practice.

Endnotes

[1] An archive that documents the works of the participant artists can be found on LARM's website: http://www.larm-festival.se/ (Accessed 19 September 2018).

[2] Documentation of the exhibition and field trips are available at: http://www.jorgenlarsson.org/index.php/en/projects/17-sleppet (Accessed 19 September 2018).

[3] A short presentation of the work installed at the Tanya Bonakdar Gallery in New York is available at: https://vimeo.com/49926863 (Accessed 19 September 2018).

[4] Recorded in Northern Canada, *The Idea of North* is the first part of Glenn Gould's *Solitude Trilogy* produced between 1967 and 1977.

[5] 'Borealism' is a term used by analogy to Orientalism as defined by Edward Saïd in 1978. Some of the recent research projects in literature studies ('Boréalisme: Pour un atlas sensible du Nord' Sorbonne University and Linköping University; 'Borealism and other Imagologies', University of Oslo) elaborated on the term as a way to describe the North as a discursive space in its relation with the South.

References

Ásdís Ólafsdóttir and Eudes, E. (2012). 'Horizonic. Art sonore – Sound art', *ARTnord Contemporary Art from the North,* 11, Paris: CHAN.

Corvese, R. (2006). *The Idea of North.* Halifax: Dalhousie University Art Gallery.

Hayashi, S. (2007). 'Art and Sound in Stockholm: New Music 2006 and LARM 2007', *Hz: Fylkingen's Net Journal.* Available at: http://www.hz-journal.org/n10/hayashi.html (Accessed: 28 August 2018).

Larsson, J. (2009). *Sleppet.* Bergen: +3db Records.

Licht, A. (2007). *Sound Art: Beyond Music, Between Categories.* New York: Rizzoli International.

Metzger, C. (2006). 'Sounds Typically German – Klangkunst', *World New Music Magazine,* 16, pp. 53-57.

Rudi, J. (2003). '*Norge - et lydrike,* Norway remixed: a sound installation', *Organised Sound,* 8(2), pp. 151-155.

Schulz, B. (2002). *Resonanzen/Resonances: Aspekte der Klangkunst/Aspects of Sound Art.* Heidelberg: Kehrer.

Søchting, R. and Kulberg, M. (2009). *Soundings: Nordic Sound Art.* Roskilde: Museet for Samtidskunst.

Toop, D. (1999). *Sonic Boom: The Art of Sound.* London: Hayward Gallery.

Mapping out Identity in the German-Danish Borderlands: New Perspectives on Hybridising Identity in National Minority Communities

Ruairidh Tarvet

Introduction

This chapter will examine the regional, national and transnational dimensions of identity in the Danish and German minorities in Schleswig. Through mapping out the history of conflict and cooperation between notions of German and Danish identity and comparing this with new data on how the minorities experience their own identity today, I will suggest that the minority communities have successfully imagined a hybridised borderland identity. The primary data gathered for this chapter were obtained from a survey study on 120 members of the Danish minority and thirty-two members of the German minority.

As national identities became more salient, in particular throughout the nineteenth century, the people of Schleswig faced a growing pressure to fully assimilate into the wider national communities. Nonetheless, many Danes and Germans who managed to preserve their ethnic identity found themselves in a minority and subject to linguistic, cultural and political influence from the majority communities. Through a history of intense contact, a high degree of interaction between minority and majority communities and a focus on bilingualism and bicultural awareness, it may be more relevant to think of ethnic identity in the minorities today as a hybrid. Not only does this identity consist of objective traits associated with Danish and German national identities but it also incorporates notions of European and regional identity. Furthermore, although membership of either minority is based on subjective affiliation, objective criteria such as language ability, cultural and social values, political views, regional connections and ancestry effectively define the group and were mentioned in the survey as important factors for inclusion by minority members. Therefore, whilst the German and Danish minorities exist as separate entities, each with their own institutions, political parties and schools, the two communities share a common interpretation of minority identity, balancing both subjective and objective components.

As communities of a borderland, the Danish and German minorities of Schleswig exhibit regional, national and transnational dimensions of social identity. Although citizenship is a clearly defined and well-regulated legal apparatus used by nation states, it does not always reflect an individual's own feelings of cultural and linguistic belonging. In the case of the German and Danish minorities, the democratic fixing of the German-Danish national border in 1920 resulted in large populations of people, claiming to be Danish- or German-minded, finding themselves no longer resident in their kin-state. As new communities in a globalising world, the minorities have had to adapt and evolve in order to survive. Today, in an era when cultural, sexual and gender identities are perceived by some to be fluid, is it also relevant to discuss ethnic identity or affiliation with a national minority as fluid or should it remain essentialist and fixed? As anyone in the borderlands can legally associate themselves subjectively with either national minority without contest, what are then the exact dimensions and dynamics of minority identity?

It is estimated that the size of the Danish minority is around 50,000 whereas the German minority has around 15,000 members

(Kühl 2005: 352). The confusion in exact size is because no single authority determines who exactly constitutes a member of either minority. Membership is polarised between debates on the subjective and objective criteria for inclusion. Indeed, the use of objective criteria by authorities to ascertain the degree of one's Danish or German identity is a contravention of the provisions set out in the Copenhagen-Bonn declarations, a set of mutual declarations made by the German and Danish states designed to protect minority rights in Schleswig (*Udenrigsministeriet* 1955). Yet objective requirements are still set by several minority institutions, such as the Danish School Union in Southern Schleswig (Dan. *Dansk Skoleforening for Sydslesvig*).

It is possible that the composite nature of self-identity in the borderlands could be a key characteristic of regional identity. In addition to national identification, transnational and regional dimensions of identity exist, consisting of elements transcending race, citizenship, ethnicity and language. In an era when physical borders are almost non-existent between Schengen states and when Germans and Danes can travel between their host and kin-states, many pre-Schengen barriers, which once reinforced the divide of ethnicity, race and nationality, have been removed with the introduction of the Schengen Agreement in 1985. Such fluidity has indeed allowed members of this borderland community to develop common social practices and norms, pass these customs on through generations and develop policies and social organisations to promote a borderland lifestyle and concept of social identity.

This chapter will seek to map out and understand the development of the regional, national and transnational dimensions of identity in the Danish and German minorities. The empirical evidence is gathered from a survey study, conducted on members of the Danish and German minorities in 2017. This evidence is then compared with developments throughout history. Through identifying and mapping out the various dimensions of identity within the Danish and German minorities, I explore the idea that the minorities exist as unique entities, where membership is perceived as consisting of hybrid national, regional and transnational identities.

A brief history of the region

In order to grasp the complex situation of identity on each side of the German-Danish border, it is essential to comprehend the background of the contact situation between Germans and Danes in the region. Medieval Schleswig was a key passage between the Northern and the Western Germanic peoples, functioning as the mainland link between Scandinavia and continental Europe (Thaler 2009: 28). Divisions became more apparent between the Northern and Western Germanic peoples around the year 806 AD. Godfred, King of Jutland, ordered the construction of the renowned defensive wall, *Danevirke*, along the river Eider as a means of fortifying Denmark's southernmost border from the encroachments of Charlemagne's ever-expanding empire. Upon the completion of *Danevirke* in 811 AD, a physical obstacle of separation lay between the two peoples, which allowed cultural and linguistic differences between the groups to thrive (Lund 2009: 61-64).

Over the following four centuries, the region of Schleswig gradually began to display traits pertaining to the emergence of a regional political authority. It was not until 1232, when King Valdemar II of Denmark (1170-1241) appointed his son Abel as Duke of Southern Jutland, that a genuine ducal lineage emerged in the area. Disputes about the extent of the Duchy's independence from the Kingdom of Denmark ensued over the course of the following century but ended with the Duchy of Southern Jutland's de-facto independence in the first half of the fourteenth century. With a now autonomous region controlled by dukes, separating the Kingdom of Denmark from Holstein, a distinct conflict of interests arose on both sides of the Duchy. In order to maintain political distance from Denmark, the dukes sought assistance from Holstein. This strengthened ties with the German-minded population. The reach of German influence was further solidified when the Schauenburg family of Holstein took over the rule of Schleswig in 1386, bringing Holstein and Schleswig under unified control. Throughout the following century, both Schleswig and Holstein remained predominantly German-speaking enclaves within the Danish kingdom (see Rasmussen, Adriansen and Madsen 2005).

Following numerous military losses to Sweden throughout the seventeenth century, Denmark lost control of Skåne and granted full autonomy to the Duchy of Schleswig, with the Gottorp dynasty assuming power. Full autonomy of the region lasted until 1720, when the Great Northern War resulted in heavy losses for the Gottorps' ally, Sweden. The Danes reassumed control of Schleswig and Holstein with the signing of the Treaty of Frederiksborg on 3 July 1720. The duchies were then governed by the German Chancellery in Copenhagen, which oversaw the administration of Danish law in the High German language (Fredsted 2003: 37). Denmark enjoyed a relatively secure control of the duchies until the early nineteenth century, as the breakup of the Holy Roman Empire in 1806 left behind uncertainties for the future of Holstein. Part of Holstein drifted more towards Denmark and the Duchy of Lauenburg joined the Kingdom following the Danish loss of Norway in 1814. This modest gain for Denmark at a time of great losses was short-lived, as both Holstein and Lauenburg were soon incorporated into the German Confederation, established by the Vienna Congress in 1815. The following decades were overshadowed by questions of nationalism and nationhood. In Kiel, the Schleswig-Holstein movement was beginning to gather momentum. Headed by Uwe Jens Lornsen, who had been inspired by the idea of German unity during his stay at the University of Jena from 1818 to 1819, the movement sought to take back financial, governmental and administrative control from Copenhagen, with the duchies to be ruled from Kiel.

On the other side of the debate, the Danish-minded population called for German and Danish equality and a unified constitution between Denmark and the duchies. A leading figure in this movement was Christian Paulsen, an academic who demanded that Danish be allowed official status in Northern Schleswig, where it was the principal spoken language. The conflict of views erupted in the form of the First Schleswig War (Dan. *Treårskrigen*), which lasted from 1848 to 1851 and ended with a Danish victory (Hjelholt 1961).

After a period of life returning to pre-war tensions, the conflicts of interest continued to grow more apparent, as Danish national-liberals called for an ever-closer union between Denmark and Schleswig. German-minded officials in Holstein and Schleswig reiterated their case for closer cooperation with the duchies within the context of a German Confederation. With the removal of Holstein and Lauenburg from the Danish constitution in 1863 and the signing of a new constitution by the Glücksburg dynasty in favour of the Danish national-liberalist cause, the Augustenburg ducal dynasty, which worked with the Schleswig-Holstein movement, restated its claim to rule of the duchies, with the intention of bringing them into the German Confederation.

In 1864, Prussia and Austria called upon Denmark to rescind its common constitution. As Denmark ignored the two nations' demands, Prussia and Austria declared war. The war marked a disaster for Denmark, which suffered heavy losses, most noticeably at the battle of Dybbøl from 7 to 18 April 1864. Following the Danish defeat at Dybbøl, Prussian and Austrian forces occupied all Northern Schleswig, thus bringing the region into Prussia.

With all of Schleswig now under Prussian control, Prussia's leader Otto von Bismarck sought to solidify German identity and language in the peripheral regions of the Prussian state. The

Danes of Schleswig found themselves under increasing pressure to assimilate into German society and become German in mind, culture and language. German was gradually introduced as the language of the school, where not only language but also history lessons became focused on Prussian regal and imperial history (Schultz Hansen 2009: 202). Alongside this, Danish unions, clubs and songs were banned and use of the term Southern Jutland (Dan. *Sønderjylland*) was forbidden. Pressures increased between the Danish-minded and German-minded Schleswigers, with families being torn apart by intercultural marriage and wavering allegiances to either side. Resentment peaked in 1914 with the outbreak of the First World War, when 35,000 men from Northern Schleswig were conscripted into the German army.

With the defeat of Germany at the end of 1918, discussions on the Schleswig question reopened. After fifty-six years of German rule in Northern Schleswig, the issue had become even more complex, with the incomplete effects of Germanisation affecting some areas more than others. Ultimately, the region was divided into two zones, with a referendum to be held in Northern Schleswig on 10 February 1920 and one in Southern Schleswig on 14 March of the same year. With a voter turnout of 91.5%, zone 1 voted 74.9% in favour of Denmark against 25.1% for Germany and zone 2 voted 80.16% in favour of Germany. The Schleswig question was widely considered to be resolved, with the majority of Schleswig's population and the international community satisfied with the smooth execution of this democratic exercise (Berdichevsky 1999: 14-17).

Following Hitler's defeat at the end of the Second World War, a large exodus of Germans and other Europeans from the former Prussian territories in the East resulted in a spike in the population size. The 1950 West German federal census reported that 37.4% (990,861 out of a total population of 2,649,192) originated from these two groups (Statistisches Landesamt Schleswig Holstein 1952). Faced with post-war hardships and a new set of challenges, the political focus in the region shifted from conflict to cooperation. As the immigrants settled and assimilated into Schleswig, the Danish and German minorities swelled in size. At the same time, the minorities solidified their status and rights with the Copenhagen-Bonn declarations and as Denmark joined the border-free Schengen Area in 2001, Schleswig began to display itself as a model for peaceful cooperation and respect for national differences and transnational identities.

Hybridising nationalisms: Religion, royals and language

Benedict Anderson identifies both religion and dynasties as the cultural roots of the nation, in what he terms the 'imagined community' (Anderson 2006 [1983]). As Christian Lutheranism is the most prevalent religious denomination across both Northern and Southern Schleswig and has been so since the Reformation, this shared transnational trait can be of use when looking at the developments in identity in the region. Both religion and ducal dynasties became intertwined during the Reformation in Schleswig, when, in the 1520s, German missionaries began to preach Martin Luther's theses in Scandinavia's major merchant ports (Grell 1994: 113). Following the conflict of the so-called Count's Feud (Dan. *Grevens fejde*), where from 1534 to 1536 Count Christoffer made an unsuccessful revolt against the King Christian III, the latter was subsequently able to solidify the role of Lutheranism and his own absolute monarchical rule in Denmark across both German and Danish speaking communities.

The harmony of religious doctrine in the region provided a common ground upon which both German and Danish-minded populations could unite, albeit within the constraints of the language of their church. The Reformation ushered in a semi-official linguistic border, through which Danish became the official language of the Church in Northern Schleswig, as did German for Southern Schleswig (Henningsen 2017: 11). This linguistic border, formed out of the former dioceses of Schleswig and Ribe, closely resembles the current political border between the two countries today, although at the time, such a border accentuated differences in loyalty within the Duchy of Schleswig. A strong link between dynastic and/or appointed power and religious authority became evident. Up until the Prussian Church reforms of 1817, the Church's sphere of influence in Southern Schleswig was guided by a distinct 'throne and altar' mentality, which it used to align itself with the Prussian government (Barnett 2006: 396). Therefore, politically, German-speaking churchgoers were highly exposed to the developments of German national thought and the political ideals which followed in the nineteenth century. Similarly, the Church in Denmark remained (and still remains) intrinsically linked to the state and the people. The Danish Church's tolerance of political activity (ibid.) arguably allowed for the expression of Danish values and later, nationalism, to seep into religious services and influence the national loyalties of the congregations.

Anderson notes that the decline in the belief of the divine nature of religious script language, hierarchy and dynastic supremacy, as well as changing perceptions of time, contributed to the imagining of nations (Anderson 2006: 36). I would argue that the linguistic divide created by state-orientated Churches and fuelled by the ducal dynasties essentially drove early notions of German and Danish nationhood in Schleswig. Although once previously united by the transnational Latin Catholic dioceses, these new divisions, created by administering the Church in the vernaculars, functioned as vehicles for national thought in the populations of Schleswig, thus enabling regional participation in the later nationalist movements of the nineteenth century.

In Schleswig, both minorities use Standard Danish or High German in official spheres as the written form, despite the differences in pronunciation, vocabulary and grammar between these and their respective vernaculars. Nonetheless, there exists an abundance of academic discussion regarding the extent to which the minorities have standardised their spoken languages. Inside the Danish minority, the uncodified dialect Southern Schleswigian Danish (Dan. *Sydslesvigdansk*) continues to function as an in-group vernacular. To define this vernacular as a mixed language would limit it to being no more than the by-product of language contact and would ignore regionally indigenous phenomena. Kurt Braunmüller suggests that the variety is instead a form of group identifier, showing both connections to, and yet distance from, the Danish varieties spoken in Denmark (Braunmüller 1991: 24).

In the German minority in Northern Schleswig, Northern Schleswigian German (Dan. *Nordslesvigtysk*) functions in a similar way, its speakers expressing their identity through the features of mixed language. Pedersen consequently terms the variety an 'ethnolect', in that its use and characteristics are limited to a particular ethnic group (Pedersen 2006: 334).

Behind such ethnolects or group identifiers lies the general attitude to language by the speakers. In the period from 1864 to 1920, the German language was enforced by the German authorities in both Northern and Southern Schleswig as the language of the Church, the school and public administration. To preserve the use of Danish in Northern Schleswig, *Sprogforeningen* was established in 1880 as a means of organising lectures and promoting literature in Danish. Language became an issue of political relevance and an indicator of national loyalty. Even after Northern Schleswig returned to Denmark in 1920, the memory of foreign rule stuck in the minds of the Danish population, who began to treat the German language with disdain. Danes distanced themselves from native German speakers, whose language they saw as evidence of a German national identity and supportive of mainstream German political trends (Pedersen 2006: 334).

Following the plebiscites in 1920, the role of language in the minorities and its implication for perceptions of national identity became contentious issues. For example, there had long been Danish-minded families who, for several generations, had supported the Danish royal family, yet due to the prestigious status of the German language had gradually adopted German as their home tongue (Pedersen 2005: 373). Beginning in 1870 and continuing into the present day, a debate on the so-called 'Language Problem' (Dan. *Sprogproblemet*) in the Danish minority is exemplified in the collection of articles, opinion pieces and letters to the editor in *Flensborg Avis*. The debate is polarised between the ideal of a solely Danish-speaking and Danish-minded minority in Southern Schleswig and the reality of a bilingual, bicultural and even primarily German-speaking Danish minority (Pedersen 2000: 263-264). With no clear consensus met outside the practices and charters of the individual minority institutions, the link between national identity and language remains an issue lacking consensus in the Danish minority.

Essential to the continuity of a shared regional identity is the narration of the minority discourse, as it is taught at home, in school and practised in daily life. Promoting this requires the continued acceptance of anyone who subjectively feels their Danish or German identity as members of that or both minorities. The minorities can be said to exist as narratives, open to association from both Schleswigers and German/Danish nationals from outside Schleswig. Their core identity is, as such, subject to eternal re-negotiation. Minority identity can equally be renounced or ignored by individuals, who otherwise could be perceived through objective means as belonging to the minorities. The minorities have therefore re-imagined their communities over the past century as open and tolerant, rooted in a regional and transnational self-understanding, yet with strong ancestral, linguistic and emotional ties to both their host and kin-states.

Minority identity in the twenty-first century

A survey study was carried out by the author of this chapter in the spring of 2017 on 120 members of the Danish minority and thirty-two members of the German minority. Participation was voluntary and advertised throughout minority institutions and newspapers. It revealed that half of the Danish minority today actively identify as Germans and Danes simultaneously. This contrasts highly with the German minority, where just 34% identify themselves as Germans and Danes simultaneously. A greater number of those claiming to be both Germans and Danes were from the younger generations. Identity labels and terminology play a pivotal role in the expression of regional identity. Danes generally tend to prefer the term 'Jutland' over 'Schleswig', as the latter has distinct German undertones and was strongly used by the German Schleswig-Holstein movement throughout the nineteenth century. Whilst 63% of the Danish minority described themselves as Schleswigian, this was only the case for 15% of the German minority. The label 'Southern Jutlandic' appealed more to the German minority, where 68% of the group assigned themselves this label, as opposed to just 32% of the Danish minority. Although both terms denote the same region, it is clear that historic usage of the terminology has impacted interpretation of the once interchangeable terms. A perception of European identity is held strongly in both minorities, where 68% of the Danish minority and 80% of the German minority stated that they felt European. It appears that European identity is easier to agree upon in both minorities than the regional identities, although the two widely co-exist.

The mixture of regional, national and transnational identities creates issues for inclusion in national contexts. Acceptance in the wider national majority populations is a problem for most of the Danish minority. Although 40% of this group felt fully accepted as part of the German national majority and 29% by the Danish national majority, most did not feel fully accepted in either. Acceptance was a slightly less salient issue for the German minority, 60% of whom feel fully accepted by the wider Danish national majority and 38% by the German national majority. Language ability cannot be regarded as the core issue here, as 98% of the Danish minority and 97% of the German minority claim that they are able to speak and write both Danish and German to a decent standard. Across both minorities, 56% of respondents regarded bilingualism as a key aspect of minority life and this is further evidenced by the fact that 64% of respondents claimed that they regularly code-switch between German and Danish in their everyday lives.

The main differences between the Danish minority and Danes in Denmark lie in the individual's accent and pronunciation of Danish as well as in their political opinion, which tends to be more in line with German national trends (especially regarding immigration policy and issues of nationalism). This is because most of the Danish minority come from predominantly German families. Speaking Danish with a German accent or so-called *Sydslesvigdansk* was perceived to be the most notable difference and for some, also a hindrance to claiming Danish identity. Similar issues were noted by the German minority, although German cultural norms such as workplace hierarchy and formalities in speech (such as use of *Sie*) were frequently cited as unfamiliar and irritating phenomena to the German minority.

It is therefore clear that the minorities are not simply displaced nationals. With their high degree of bilingualism and an understanding of both national cultures, members are able to cherry-pick opinions, traits, cultural practices, political views and even linguistic capital from both nations. Although this cherry-picking may draw upon banal aspects of daily life, it allows for the creation and negotiation of a distinct regional identity within the minority social spheres, in other words, a hybrid identity. The minorities are thus communities in their own right, comprising elements from both nations and a shared region. Although they are national minorities, their existence depends on a deep sense of regional belonging.

Conclusion

In the absence of conflict or tensions between the nations, the notion of regional identity can act as a bridge between national differences and foster a sense of dual nationalism. The survey underlined both the duality as well as the hybridity of national identity. Duality exists in that it is possible for Danish and German identities to live side by side and co-exist within similar domains, such as at home, in school and in public life. Hybridity of national identity can also be said to be the case, as language attitudes, the mixing of cultural practices and cherry-picking of political and social ideals from both nations results in a unique minority identity, different from that of either nation. The diffusion of linguistic and cultural material from two almost equidistant capital centres, combined with diffusion on a local scale, has emboldened this duality and hybridity. It is clear from the results that neither hybrid nor dual national identities are mutually exclusive and both can be experienced by the same individual simultaneously. Fundamental to realising this possibility is the notion that national loyalties are not necessarily singular and that a common European identity highlights similarities rather than differences. It is therefore possible to identify as a German and a Dane at the same time, grounding justification in the historical complexity of Schleswig and expressing this duality in one's everyday interactions. Individuals who did not reside in Schleswig felt that they had 'lost' their justification to claim minority identity, emphasising the regional basis for the duality and hybridity of national identity.

Given the promotion of inclusiveness and tolerance, as well as the encouragement of a multi-cultural and multi-linguistic community, one could be led to assume that the minorities represent a form of civic nationalism or, indeed, civic regionalism. To draw such a conclusion would, however, ignore the fact that these communities are deeply rooted in an ethnic bedrock of language, history and culture. Without connections to the region, proficiency in either German or Danish and/or knowledge of the cultural practices of the communities, membership of either minority would be greatly impeded due to the requirements of the minority institutions and the general expectations of the communities' members. Therefore, whilst the minorities exhibit clearly civic, inclusive, tendencies in their nationalism and regionalism, they are still dependent on certain ethnic interpretations of their social identity in order to authenticate their self-understanding and justify a kinship to both nations.

With membership officially based on subjective will, these two interpretations clash. This clash is highlighted by the difficulties faced by minority members in acceptance by majority national communities. In such situations, it is not subjective will which divides the minorities from their majority counterparts; rather it is the presence of objective differences in accent, political opinion, cultural practices and language choice which prevents full acceptance. Wedged between two uncertain national belongings, the minorities root themselves in the region and the transnation, which promote diversity and inclusion, yet members still practise the language, culture and traditions of both nations. This is not to say that constructivism has not played a role. Indeed, everything which distinguishes the minorities from their kin-state counterparts, in particular language (accent, bilingualism, code-switching) and the practice of hybridised cultures, represents the impact of social constructivism on minority group identity.

To utilise Brubaker's integrative approach to defining ethnicity (Brubaker 2004: 85), it becomes clear that a balance must be struck between the primordial interpretation of the minorities as historically-grounded groups and the present-day reality of the groups having developed distinct and unique characteristics since their official recognition. The minorities can be regarded as supplementary communities to the national majorities, offering an alternative or additional national identity and a third space in which to cherry-pick the most advantageous aspects of social, cultural and linguistic capital from both nations. In doing so, the minorities have married their kin-state and host state national identities, thereby reimagining their own social identity.

Given that there exists a clear dispute between objective and subjective interpretations of minority identity, it is necessary to encompass both approaches. Throughout history, ethnic identity in Schleswig has been tested and re-defined through regional, national and transnational conflict and cooperation. As such, the minorities, as both essentialist and constructed groups, can only be the product of a collective imagination. They are no longer simply displaced nationals residing in a neighbouring land as a result of the redrawing of national borders, nor are they interested in forming a nation of their own. Instead, they are two, closely-linked communities sustained by a shared will to maintain their distinctiveness.

References

Anderson, B. (2016 [1983]). *Imagined Communities: Reflections on the Origin and Spread of Nationalism*, Brooklyn: Verso.

Barnett, V. (2006). 'The Lutheran Churches' in Blamires, C. (ed.): *World Fascism: A Historical Encyclopedia*, Vol 1, Santa Barbara: ABC-CLIO, pp. 396-397.

Berdichevsky, N. (1999). *The German-Danish Border: The Successful Resolution of an Age Old Conflict or its Redefinition?*, Durham: Durham University.

Braunmüller, K. (1991). 'Sydslesvigdansk — et blandingssprog?', *Mål & Mæle*, 4, pp. 24-29.

Brubaker, R. (2004). *Ethnicity Without Groups*, Cambridge: Harvard University Press.

Fredsted, E. (2003). 'Language Contact and Bilingualism in Flensburg in the Middle of the 19th Century', in Braunmüller, K. and Ferraresi, G. (eds): *Aspects of Multilingualism in European Language History*, Amsterdam: John Benjamins Publishing, pp. 35-59.

Grell, O. P. (1994). 'Scandinavia', in Scribner, R., Porter, R. and Teich, M. (eds): *The Reformation in National Context*, Cambridge: Cambridge University Press, pp. 111-130.

Henningsen, L. (2017). *En festhilsen i anledning af 500 året for reformationen: til det danske mindretal fra dets kirke*, Flensburg: Dansk Kirke i Sydslesvig.

Hjelholt, H. (1961). *Sønderjylland under treårskrigen; fra foråret 1849 til freden med Preussen juli 1850: et bidrag til dets politiske historie*, Vol 2, Copenhagen: Gads forlag.

Kühl, J. (2005). 'Die Organisationen der dänischen Minderheit', in Kühl, J. and Bohn, R. (eds): *Ein europäisches Modell?: Nationale Minderheiten im deutsch-dänischen Grenzland 1945-2005*, Gütersloh: Verlag für Regionalgeschichte, pp. 341-377.

Lund, N. (2009). 'Danewerke', in Fryde, N., and Reitz, D. (eds): *Walls, Ramparts and Lines of Demarcation: Selected Studies from Antiquity to Modern Times*, Münster: LIT Verlag, pp. 57-65.

Pedersen, K. M. (2000). *Dansk sprog i Sydslesvig*, Vol 2, Aabenraa: Institut for Grænseregionsforskning.

Pedersen, K. M. (2005). 'Realiteter og Rettigheder inden for Sprog og Identitet – i det Danske og Tyske Mindretal før og efter København-Bonn Erklæringerne i 1955', in Kühl, J. (ed.), *København-Bonn Erklæringerne 1955-2005. De Danske Mindretalserklæringers Baggrund, Tilblivelse og Virkning*, Aabenraa: Institut for Grænseregionsforskning, pp. 339-399.

Pedersen, K. M. (2006). 'Sprogbrug og sprogsyn hos flertal og mindretal i den dansk-tyske grænseregion', *Nordiske Studier i Leksikografi*, 8, pp. 323-346.

Rasmussen, C. P., Adriansen, I. and Madsen, L. S. (eds.) (2005). *De slesvigske hertuger*, Aabenraa: Historisk Samfund for Sønderjylland.

Schultz Hansen, H. (2009). 'Nationalitetskamp og modernisering 1815-1918', in Schultz Hansen, H. and Becker-Christensen, H. (eds): *Sønderjyllands historie efter 1815: 2*, Aabenraa: Historisk Samfund for Sønderjylland, pp. 91-93.

Statistisches Landesamt Schleswig Holstein (1952). *Statistisches Jahrbuch Schleswig-Holstein*.

Thaler, P. (2009). *Of Mind and Matter: The Duality of National Identity in the German-Danish Borderlands*, West Lafayette: Purdue University Press.

Udenrigsministeriet (1955) = *København-Bonn Erklæringerne af 29. marts 1955*. Available at: https://www.graenseforeningen.dk/leksikon/koebenhavn-bonn (Last accessed: 7 January 2019).

MYTHOLOGICAL HOMES

Which way to Jǫtunheimar? A study of the multiple realms of the Jǫtnar

Blake Middleton

The interactions between the Æsir (gods) and Jǫtnar (giants) form the core antagonistic narrative throughout the poems and prose narratives of the Old Norse mythological tradition (Clunies Ross 1994: 56-60, 75-79). During these narrative interactions, both the Æsir and Jǫtnar travel to each other's lands repeatedly, such as Þórr and Loki traveling to Jǫtunheimar (Lands of the Jǫtnar) in *Þrymskviða* 20-21 or the arrival of three þursar meyjar (giant maidens) at Ásgarðr from Jǫtunheimar in *Vǫluspá* 8. However, while conventional mythic readings tend to view the Jǫtnar as the more aggressive and invasive of the two, it is only at Ragnarǫk[1] that the Jǫtnar's movement towards the Æsir is in any way an overt aggressive act, as upon arrival the two forces will go to war. Indeed, the Eddic sources repeatedly note, for example, that Þórr is 'í austrvegi' (in the east) smashing Trǫll (trolls) and Gýgjar (giantesses).[2] Similarly, other Æsir such as Óðinn, or servants of the Æsir, such as Skírnir, enter Jǫtunheimar with the express purpose of taking objects and female Jǫtnar/Gýgjar and using them as the Æsir see fit.

Nevertheless, this chapter does not discuss these narrative conflicts; instead, it focuses on providing insights into the detailed descriptions of a number of the various locations in, and associated with, Jǫtunheimar and its inhabitants, in which the Eddic narratives occur. In doing so, some of the general traits and motifs associated with the Jǫtnar will be presented.

Cosmology and world view in pre-Christian Norse societies

In response to the question: 'Hvernig var jǫrðin háttuð?' (How was the earth arranged?) in *Gylfaginning* chapter 8, *Snorra Edda*[3] provides some rudimentary, mythological cosmography:

> Hon er kringlótt útan, ok flar útan um liggr hinn djúpi sjár, ok með þeiri sjávar strǫndu gáfu þeir lǫnd til bygðar jǫtna ættum. En fyrir innan á jǫrðunni gerði þeir borg umhverfis heim fyrir ófriði jǫtna, en til þeirar borgar hǫfðu þeir brár Ymis jǫtuns, ok kǫlluðu þá borg Miðgarð. (*Gylfaginning*: 12).

> (It is circular round the edge, and around it lies the deep sea, and along the shore of this sea they gave lands to live in to the races of giants. But on the earth on the inner side they made a fortification round the world [of men] against the hostility of the giants, and for this fortification they used the giant Ymir's eyelashes, and they called the fortification Midgard.) (Faulkes 1987: 2-3).

In addition, per *Gylfaginning* 9, following the creation of these two locations the 'Æsir gerðu þeir sér borg í miðjum heimi er kallaðr er Ásgarðr' (*Gylfaginning*: 13) (made themselves a city in the middle of the world which is known as Asgard, Faulkes 1987: 13). From these passages a 'basic, fairly well-accepted model' of the Eddic universe is identified (Steinsland 2005: 138), one in which these three localities are situated on a flat, horizontal plane of undetermined breadth;[4] with the realms of Ásgarðr and Miðgarðr featuring fortified boundaries meant to keep the Jǫtnar out, and the area outside said barriers constituting the realm of Jǫtunheimar.

As spatial orientation plays an important role in the Eddic narratives (Clunies Ross 1994: 50-56), most acutely here in the placement of the Jǫtnar in a distant location in the mythological landscape, a brief examination of scholarly models of the Eddic landscape's layout will be presented. In previous decades, scholars have toiled to elucidate how the pre-Christian Norse perceived the Eddic landscape and how that cosmological model might have intersected with real world locations.[5] Many of these studies examine this cosmological layout from an anthropological point of view, presenting a structurally binary model of said cosmos; one focused on the dichotomy of being either 'innangarðs' (inside the fence [or enclosure]) or 'útangarðs' (outside the fence) (Gurevich 1969: 43). To this were integrated notions of cultural semantic oppositions, such as culture-nature, life-death, or familiar-alien (Meletinskij 1973: 46-48; Meletinskij 1977: 251-252), resulting in the unification of Miðgarðr and Ásgarðr into one location and juxtaposing this unified realm with that of Jǫtunheimar (Hastrup 1990: 26-27).[6] In dividing the mythic world between these opposing concepts, Kirsten Hastrup additionally assigns the inhabitants into similar opposing social groups, a familiar group 'inside the fence' – an 'us' – and those who lived 'outside the fence' – someone 'other' (1990: 34), that is, the Æsir and Jǫtnar, respectively.

This landscape division has, however, been contested by other scholars, including Margaret Clunies Ross (1994) and Gro Steinsland (2005). For Steinsland, the assimilation of Ásgarðr and Miðgarðr removes all sense of the Æsir's significance – their central place in the cosmos and even their very divinity. Further, by likewise combining mankind with the Æsir, Miðgarðr loses its intended meaning as a liminal space between the two opposing supernatural forces (2005: 141).

For Clunies Ross, the preferred interpretation of the horizontal axis is one divided into three, forming 'a series of concentric half-circles': the innermost 'half-circle' being home to the Æsir, Álfar (elves), and mankind; the middle area as the dominion of the Jǫtnar and Dvergar (dwarves); and the outermost location as home to a proposed third major group of supernatural beings (Clunies Ross

1994: 51). While Clunies Ross's division alleviates some problems, it also creates some potential issues. In particular, the characters Útgarðaloki (Útgarðr's Loki) and the Miðgarðsormr (Miðgarðr's serpent), are interpreted as 'supernatural beings who represent natural forces that are not susceptible to social control' rather than as 'ordinary giants' (Clunies Ross 1994: 51). This is not a view I adhere to, as both beings are expressly labelled in the *Eddas* as being Jǫtnar. Additionally, like the previous model, Clunies Ross's organisation of the horizontal axis limits the importance and divine nature of the Æsir, as well as weakening the 'otherness' of the Jǫtnar by effectively placing them in the middle.

By placing the Jǫtnar in the outermost area, the beings are linked to expanses of the landscape which remain untamed; lands which Hastrup remarks were conceived as being highly dangerous, whereas the lands 'inside the yard' were familiar and secure (1990: 28). Therefore, the Jǫtnar are both outside the control of the Æsir and beyond the limits of mankind's social organisation, and as the narrative of the *Eddas* are told from the perspective of the Æsir (Clunies Ross 1994: 49), the Jǫtnar must naturally assume the role of dangerous 'outsiders' to the Æsir and mankind's friendly 'insiders'.

In his assessment of mythological space, Aron Gurevich noted that it was 'devoid of fixed topographical identity' (1969: 46). While this sentiment might hold true for the initial description of localities such as Jǫtunheimar, which, beyond being placed along the shore of a deep sea, is only additionally described as both mountainous and barren, descriptions of particular places are developed more fully in the Eddic poems. However, despite these more detailed descriptions, in *Gylfaginning* 8 there remains uncertainty of where 'hinn djúpi sjár' (the deep sea) (*Gylfaginning*: 12) is in relation to the two realms of Miðgarðr and Jǫtunheimar. Are the territories contiguous or are the lands of the Jǫtnar separated from Miðgarðr and Ásgarðr by the sea?

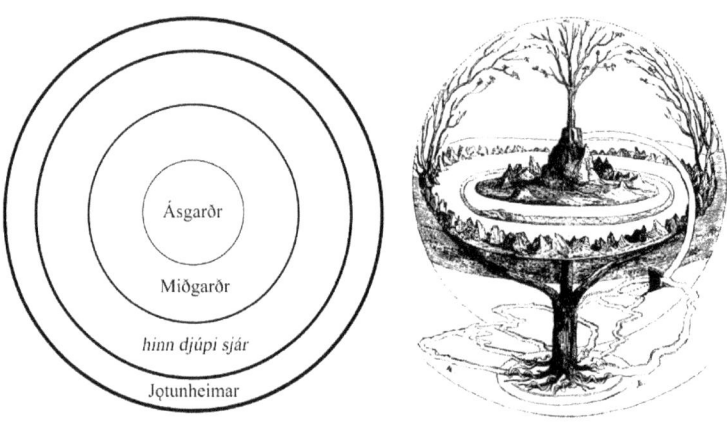

Fig. 1: *Left: Overhead view of Option A of the Eddic cosmos. Illustration and Copyright: Middleton 2019. Right: Copy of illustration of Yggdrasill in Finnur Magnússon 1825: 340. Copyright: Public Domain.*

Beginning with the latter (which I will here call 'Option A'), an interpretation of the sea acting as a divider between the land of both men and Æsir, and those of the Jǫtnar, is found in *Gylfaginning* 45: '[Þórr] byrjaði ferðina austr í Jǫtunheima ok allt til hafsins, ok þá fór hann út yfir hafit þat it djúpa. En er hann kom til lands þá gekk hann upp [...].' (*Gylfaginning*: 37) ([Þórr] started on his journey east to Giantland and all the way to the sea, and then he went out across the great deep sea. And when he reached land he went ashore [...].) (Faulkes 1987: 38).

This statement, which notes the existence of something beyond the water, contradicts *Gylfaginning* 8's statement, leaving the *Snorra Edda* reader to interpret whether this land beyond is understood to be a part of Jǫtunheimar, or something entirely separate and altogether more frightening, akin to Clunies Ross's model (Clunies Ross 1994: 51-52, 265-268).

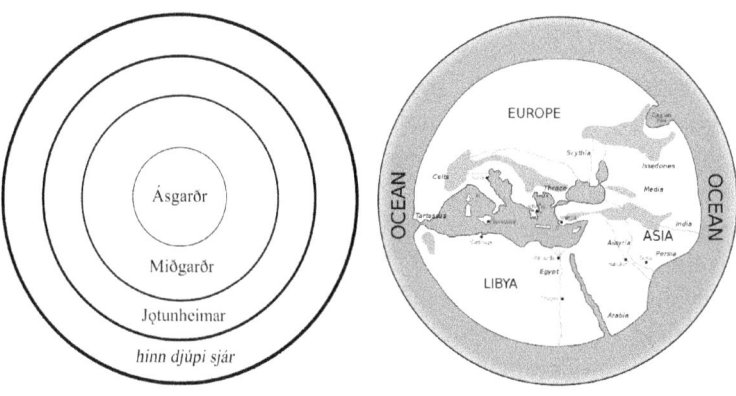

Fig. 2: *Left: Overhead view of Option B of the Eddic cosmos. Illustration and Copyright: Middleton 2019. Right: reproduction of Hecatæus' map circa 500 BC. Copyright: Public Domain.*

This separation of Jǫtunheimar from the remainder of the mythic world, while logical, likewise contradicts other motifs which intricately intertwine with the narratives, such as the association of Jǫtunheimar with 'austrit' (the east) (Rösli 2015: 146-166). However, if the cosmological model of Old Norse speakers were akin to Fig. 1, then the Jǫtnar would be all encompassing of the inner landmass, and while the narratives do suggest the Jǫtnar will arrive from many directions, there is never any suggestion that they will advance from 'vestrit' (the west).

Conversely, if the territories of the Jǫtnar and mankind were joined together in one large landmass (here called 'Option B'), then *Gylfaginning* 8 renders the world into a state similar to the map attributed to Hecatæus of Miletus (*c.* 550 BC–*c.* 476 BC) (Fig. 2, on the right),[7] where all available land is contiguous and surrounded by the sea, which forms the boundary for the world.

This interpretation is dependent on the importance, and purpose, of the 'deep sea' as well as its occupant, the Miðgarðsormr. The latter is repeatedly presented in kennings ('a nominal periphrasis'[8]) as something to the effect of the belt of the world: 'Moldþinur' (earth-rope) (Vǫluspá 58: 3); 'umgjǫrð allra landa' (all-lands-girdler) (Hymiskviða 22: 7-8); 'men storðar' (necklace of the earth) (Húsdrápa 3 in Marold 2017: 412-413); and Gylfaginning 47 relates the snake-shaped 'jǫtunn liggr um lǫnd ǫll' (lies encircling all lands) (Gylfaginning: 43). The repeated utilisation of this 'world-encircler' motif cannot be ignored and suggests that this was the predominant view of the mythological material.

Homesteads of the giants:
Specific locations related to the Jǫtnar

Having examined the potential geographical layout of the Norse cosmos's horizontal axis, this chapter will now turn its attention to the discussion of a selection of locations in, neighbouring, or connected to Jǫtunheimar. These are locations which are similar to the world surrounding the skalds and their audiences: the Eddas tell of rivers, seas, straits, mountains, meadows, and farms. And, though the majority of that landscape is to be found in descriptions of the territories of the Æsir and of mankind, these descriptions also serve as landmarks in the lands of the Jǫtnar.

The name of the first location discussed, Útgarðr (outer-enclosure) recalls the previously discussed social and legal concept of being 'outside the fence', or outside the lawfully structured domain of mankind. According to Vilhelm Grønbech, the location was an endless wasteland, which requires more than the normal amount of strength, wisdom, and grit to return from alive (1931: 176-179). On this matter, Lukas Rösli notes that other early discussions of the locale interpreted the Jǫtnar in an unspoken, yet highly recognisably xenophobic manner; equating the Jǫtnar who dwelt in Útgarðr to a foreign, barbaric, man-eating group who held a strong association with the dead (2017: 213-214).

Of the locations found inside Jǫtunheimar, Útgarðr provides the most details concerning said -garðr's (enclosure) location and description, despite only being cited in *Gylfaginning* chapters 45-48 (Clunies Ross 1994: 51), wherein it is stated that Útgarðr lies east of Miðgarðr – specifically east of the farmstead of Þórr's servants Þjalfi and Rǫskva – beyond 'the deep sea'. Furthermore, Útgarðr was a two-and-a-half-day journey beyond this sea, through a sizeable forest (*Gylfaginning*: 37) to a 'wide and beautiful open landscape' on which the enclosure sat (*Gylfaginning*: 43). As for the 'borg' (fortification) itself, its gates were noted to be heavy and immovable, even for Þórr, and had a high curtain wall. Inside its walls, *Gylfaginning* notes that Útgarðr had a great hall similar to those found in Ásgarðr, one that included hearths, benches, and a high-seat. Finally, regarding its appearance, or lack thereof, *Gylfaginning* 47 relates that Útgarðr, most likely through Útgarðaloki's magic, was capable of disappearing or possibly physically moving from one location to another.[9]

Þrymheimr (noisy home) (Simek 1993: 330) was at one time the home of the jǫtunn Þjazi, before being passed to his daughter Skaði:

Þrymheimr heitir inn sétti er Þjazi bjó, sá inn ámáttki jǫtunn; en nú Skaði byggvir, skír brúðr goða, fornar tóptir fǫður. (*Grímnismál* 11).	(Thrymheim the sixth is called, where Thiazi lived, the all-powerful giant; but now Skadi, the shining bride of the gods, lives in her father's ancient courts.) (Larrington 2014: 50).

The location's name also suggests that the jǫtunn Þrymr had, at one time, called the location home. However, as noted by John

Lindow (2001: 293) and Rudolf Simek (1993: 330), the names are not necessarily connected, especially considering that there is no known connection between the two in either *Edda* (Lindow 2001: 293). Concerning its location, *Skáldskaparmál* G56 (*Gylfaginning* epilogue) relates that the 'ancient courts' of Þjazi were located somewhere north of Ásgarðr and were relatively close to open water, as Þjazi was able to go fishing on the sea (*Skáldskaparmál*: 2). This sentiment is also found in *Gylfaginning* 23, where it suggests that the sea and Þrymheimr must have been in reasonably close proximity, as Skaði and her husband Njǫrðr (a sea-god) agree to alternate between his home Nóatún, located next to the sea, and her inherited abode, located amongst the snow-covered mountains, every nine days.[10]

Although *Skáldskaparmál* provides no information as to any inhabitants of Þrymheimr, save for Þjazi, Skaði, and for a short time the goddess Iðunn after she was abducted by Þjazi, *Þrymskviða* states that numerous Jǫtnar once occupied Þrymr's hall, but were all killed by Þórr.[11] Additionally, Þrymr's hall was noted to have benches and extensive amounts of treasures and luxuries, and it was well stocked with livestock, fish, baked goods, and various alcoholic beverages (*Þrymskviða* 22-24).

The distance from Ásgarðr to Þrymheimr, again if related to Þrymr, was at least eight days' travel, as noted by Loki's replies to Þrymr:

Át vætr Freyja átta nóttum, svá var hon óðfús í jǫtunheima. (*Þrymskviða* 26: 5-8).	(Freyja ate nothing for eight nights, so madly eager was she to come to Giant-land.) (Larrington 2014: 96).

Svaf vætr Freyja	(Freyja did not sleep for
átta nóttum,	eight nights,
svá var hon óðfús	so madly eager was she to
í jǫtunheima.	come to Giant-land.)
(*Þrymskviða* 28: 5-8).	(Larrington 2014: 97).

Muspellsheimr (Muspell's world/home), or simply Muspell, is one of two locations (discussed in this chapter) narratively connected with Jǫtunheimar, yet not inside it. The -heimr form of the location's name only appears in *Gylfaginning* chapters 4, 7, and 10, and is generally interpreted to attribute ownership/control of the realm to an eponymous jǫtunn called Muspell.[12] However, as *Snorra Edda* uses Muspell interchangeably with Muspellsheimr, and due to multiple 'heiti' (poetic synonym[s]),[13] including 'Muspells megir' (Muspell's might) (*Gylfaginning* 12, 50), 'Muspells lýðir' (Muspell's people) (*Vǫluspá* 49), and 'Muspells synir' (Muspell's sons) (*Lokasenna* 42, *Gylfaginning* 3, 4, 12, 36, 43, and 50), the term Muspell should be regarded as a place-name rather than as an otherwise unknown jǫtunn (Simek 1993: 222-223; Lindow 2001: 234).

In keeping with the motif of opposites presented in the spatial models above, according to Snorri in *Gylfaginning* 4,[14] Muspellsheimr was one of two diametrically opposed locations mysteriously created before the formation of the proto-jǫtunn Ymir. Snorri placed the realm in the south and implied it to be continuously alight:

Fyrst var þó sá heimr í suðrhálfu er Muspell heitir. Hann er ljóss ok heitr. Sú átt er logandi ok brennandi, er hann ok ófœrr þeim er þar eru útlendir ok eigi eigu þar óðul. (*Gylfaginning*: 9).

(First there was the world in the southern region called Muspell. It is bright and hot. That area is flaming and burning and it is impassable for those that are foreigners there and are not native to it.) (Faulkes 1987: 9).

Very little is retained in the available sources as to any geographical features or individual inhabitants save the placement of the -heimr across the sea from Ásgarðr, as noted in the first half of *Vǫluspá* 49:

Kjóll ferr austan,	(A ship journeys from the
koma munu Múspells um lǫg lýðir,	east, Muspell's troops are coming
en Loki stýrir;	over the ocean, and Loki steers.)
(*Vǫluspá* 49: 1-4).	(Larrington 2014: 10).

The indication that the 'Muspells lýðir' require the use of a boat reflects an understanding that Muspellsheimr lies outside of the cosmos's central landmass in a similar fashion to the interpretation of Jǫtunheimar in 'Option A' above. Furthermore, while this interpretation might have been the predominant rendering by the Eddic audience, *Vǫluspá* 49 complicates matters by including the ship's embarkation point as being 'ferr austan' (journeys from the east). As noted previously, the east is generally associated with snow-covered, craggy mountains and dense forests, not the flames and molten detritus of Snorri's Muspellsheimr. Moreover, the appearance of Muspell's troops in the east is confusing, considering the notation in *Vǫluspá* 51 that 'Surtr ferr sunnan / með sviga lævi' (Surt comes from the south with branches-ruin [sword/flame]) (*Vǫluspá* 51: 1-2; Larrington 2014: 10).

Lastly, adjacent to Jǫtunheimar was the realm known, interchangeably, as either Hel (realm of the dead), Niflhel (mist-Hel), or Niflheimr (mist-world). *Gylfaginning* 34 narrates that Hel (the ruler of the realm) was cast into Niflheimr where she took possession of those who died of infirmity and old age (*Gylfaginning*: 27).[15] As noted previously, Niflheimr is regarded as one of two primordial realms to predate all other locales or beings in Snorri's *Gylfaginning*. Furthermore, as noted by its toponym, the realm was to be interpreted as a contrasting world of cold and damp (via the implied mist) to the endless fire of Muspellheimr. When applying one of the realm's other names – Hel – we must then note that unlike many interpretations of the similarly sounding Christian locale, the Old Norse realm was not a place associated with the collection and torture of sinners. In its earliest form 'hel' simply meant 'to cover, hide, or conceal' primarily in the sense of a dead body (Ellis-Davidson 1968: 83-84).

Of particular interest to the current discussion is the description of Hermóðr's[16] ride to Hel's kingdom with the express hope of returning to Ásgarðr with Baldr after the latter's death (*Gylfaginning* 49). Hermóðr rode for nine nights from Ásgarðr, through ever darkening and deep forests, to the river Gjǫll and its bridge Gjallarbrú (Gjǫll's bridge) (*Gylfaginning*: 47), which borders the underworld. Upon arrival at the golden bridge, Hermóðr encountered the maiden Móðguðr, who acts as the crossing's guardian and provides the god with further directions to Hel's domain, remarking 'niðr ok norðr liggr Helvegr' (downward and northward lies the road to Hel) (*Gylfaginning*: 47). This confirms the direction noted in *Baldrs draumar* 2, wherein Óðinn proceeds on Sleipnir 'reið hann niðr þaðan / Niflheljar til' (down from there he rode to Mist-hell) (*Baldrs draumar* 2: 5-6; Larrington 2014: 235), whilst also providing a horizontal direction to the already established vertical.

Conclusions

The above discussions of the research history regarding the spatial orientation of the mythic landscape and the literary analysis of the multiple named locations associated with the Jǫtnar has shown that while the positioning of many of those locations are straightforward in a topographic sense — some Jǫtnar live in the east, such as Útgarðaloki; some live in the north, such as Þrymr — others are vague, contradictory, and confusing. Some of the issues with these locations may spawn from the contradictory information provided by the preserved sources, such as the location of Muspellsheimr, noted in *Snorra Edda* as being in the south, whilst *Vǫluspá* suggests the embarkation point of 'Muspells lýðir' is in the east. Other locations might be considered confusing because they are both on the horizontal and vertical axes, such as Hel; and others still are left untethered to any specific location, simply somewhere 'out there' (Clunies Ross 1994: 54), because of the limited available knowledge and the vagueness of the materials that are available, such as with the location of Þjazi and Skaði's mountain abode, if it is regarded as separate from Þyrmr's hall.

Regardless, while the directionality of these locations is not always easily interpreted, the territories and dwelling places themselves are far less confusing or contradictory. While details may be vague, each of the locations is described using images and objects familiar to the Eddic audiences: forests, bodies of water, plains; halls with furniture, food, libations, and on occasion social communities. As such, while the Jǫtnar are 'other', 'foreign' and on occasion embodiments of chaos, they are grounded in locales that anchor them to the 'real world', albeit places that, from the descriptions invoked in the *Eddas*, no early-medieval Scandinavian should ever consider going.

Endnotes

[1] According to Lindow (2001: 254-258), Ragnarǫk (fate/judgement of the gods/powers) is a doomsday event, prophesised to eventually occur in the Old Norse mythic future. The event will include the deaths of the majority of the gods, along with both their enemies (the Jǫtnar) and the destruction of the cosmos – which will subsequently reappear along with a select few gods.

[2] 'The east' is used in several Eddic poems and prose passages to denote the general direction in which the Jǫtnar reside.

[3] According to *SkP* ([1]: cv-cxv), *Snorra Edda* is one of two primary sources which recount Old Norse mythology; the other is the *Poetic Edda*. *Snorra Edda* is prosemetric in composition, and consists of four sections: a Prologue, *Gylfaginning* (The tricking of Gylfi [a legendary Swedish king]), *Skáldskaparmál* (The language of poetry), and *Háttatal* (Enumeration of verse-forms). *Gylfaginning* recounts the myths in prose with citations to relevant *Poetic Edda* poem stanzas, *Skáldskaparmál* serves as a sourcebook of poetic heiti and kennings (see notes 8 and 13) with numerous references to Skaldic poetry (see Simek 1993: 287-288 for brief overview), and *Háttatal* is a poem (with prose commentary) in which ninety-five different Old Norse poetic verse-forms are described.

[4] In addition to this horizontal plane was a vertical axis, which was expressed most clearly through the 'mjǫtvið mæran' (mighty measure-tree) (*Vǫluspá* 2: 7) called Yggdrasill, an *axis mundi* which linked the land of the living (Miðgarðr) with two lands of the dead, Valhǫll (hall of the slain) and Hel (the land of the 'ordinary' and dishonourable dead). However, this chapter will only focus on the horizontal axis. For discussion of the vertical axis, see Schjødt (1990).

[5] See, for example, Gurevich (1969), Meletinskij (1977), and Steinsland (2005).

[6] Many analyses of the mythic landscape, including Hastrup and Meletinskij, incorrectly refer to Útgarðr (outer-enclosure) as a synonym for the entire realm of Jǫtunheimar. This is however wrong, as Útgarðr is, rather, only one of the many locations found inside Jǫtunheimar. For further background on this interpretation and its inaccuracy, see Schjødt (1990), Brink (2004), and Rösli (2015; 2017).

[7] Hecataeus of Miletus was an early Greek historian, mythographer, and geographer who produced one of the earliest comprehensive treatises

concerning the physical layout of the (then) known-world.

[8] See *SkP* ([1]: lxvii), consisting of a base-word and one or more determinants.

[9] In addition to this, Rösli (2015: 166-174) highlights the different narrative use of Útgarðr in *Gylfaginning* from the Eddic poetry. Therein Rösli highlights the overtly oversized features of the locale as elements which are created by the three Æsir speakers as a part of a larger false narrative to trick their guest Gylfi.

[10] It should be noted that the number of days spent at each location need not likewise reflect the time travelled between the two. It is presumed that the intended constant relocation of the couple would necessitate their proximity to one another, as it is unlikely that either would wish to endure prolonged travel every one-and-a-half weeks.

[11] The Eddic poem *Þrymskviða* recounts how Þórr's hammer was stolen by Þrymr and only retrieved through an act of trickery. Once Þórr retrieved his mallet, his first act was to kill all Jǫtnar present.

[12] Rösli (2015: 153-154) notes that the uncertainty of whether Muspell was indicative of an individual or a proper-toponym was irrelevant as the term is used as the starting point of the action, which is merely recounted to present a vague location of the impending threat from somewhere 'outside'.

[13] See *SkP* (3 [1]: 1xvii), a heiti is an alternative and often descriptive term or name used for a frequently-occurring object or person mentioned in eddic and skaldic poetry, e.g. 'Skævaðr' (high-strider) for 'horse', or 'Yggr', an alternative name for the god Óðinn.

[14] Though this chapter follows the convention of naming Snorri Sturluson as the author of the eponymous *Snorra Edda*, scholarship is still uncertain of Snorri's authorship of the various texts attributed to him. For further discussion, see Wanner (2008: 26-29) and Heimir Pálsson (2017).

[15] Niflheimr spans both the horizontal and vertical. As related to the horizontal, Hel's domain is regarded as lying in the north and was one of only two things to exist prior to the forming of Ymir or the cosmos; the other being Muspellheimr.

[16] According to Lindow (2001: 173), Hermóðr is a lesser member of the Æsir and brother to Baldr.

References

Baldrs Draumar = Jónas Kristjánsson, Vésteinn Ólason and Þórður Ingi Guðjónsson (eds.) (2014). *Eddukvæði*, 2 vols, Reykjavík: Hið íslenzka fornritafélag.

Brink, S. (2004). 'Mytologiska rum och eskatologiska föreställningar i det vikingatida Norden', in Andrén, A. Jennbert, K., and Raudvere, C. (eds.) *Ordning mot kaos: Studier av nordisk forkristen kosmologi*, Lund: Nordic Academic Press, pp. 291-316.

Clunies Ross, M. (1994). *Prolonged Echoes: Old Norse Myths in Medieval Northern Society. Volume 1: The Myths*, Odense: Odense University Press.

Ellis-Davidson, H. (1968). *The Road to Hel: A Study of the Conception of the Dead in Old Norse Literature*, New York: Greenwood Press.

Faulkes, A. (trans.) (1987). *Snorri Sturluson, Edda*, London: Everyman.

Finnur Magnússon. (1825). *Eddalæren og dens Oprindelse eller Nöjagtig Fremstilling af de gamle Nordboeres Digtninge og Meninger om Verdens, Gudernes, Aandernes og Menneskenes Tilblivelse, Natur og Skjæbne*, vol 3, Copenhagen: Gyldendalske Boghandling.

Gylfaginning = Faulkes, A. (ed.) (2005). *Snorri Sturluson, Edda. Prologue and Gylfaginning*, Exeter: Viking Society for Northern Research.

Grímnismál = Jónas Kristjánsson, Vésteinn Ólason and Þórður Ingi Guðjónsson (eds.) (2014). *Eddukvæði*, 2 vols, Reykjavík: Hið íslenzka fornritafélag.

Grønbech, V. (1931). *The Culture of the Teutons*, 2 vol, trans. by Worster, W., London: Oxford University Press.

Gurevich, A. Y. (1969). 'Space and time in the *Weltmodell* of the old Scandinavian peoples', *Mediaeval Scandinavia*, 2, pp. 42-53.

Hastrup, K. (1990). *Island of Anthropology: Studies in Past and Present Iceland*, Odense: Odense University Press.

Heimir Pálsson. (2017). 'Reflections on the Creation of Snorri Sturluson's Prose Edda', *Scripta Islandica*, 68, pp. 189-232.

Hymiskviða = Jónas Kristjánsson, Vésteinn Ólason and Þórður Ingi Guðjónsson (eds.) (2014). *Eddukvæði*, 2 vols, Reykjavík: Hið íslenzka fornritafélag.

Larrington, C. (trans.) (2014). *The Poetic Edda*, Oxford and New York: Oxford University Press.

Lindow, J. (2001). *Norse Mythology: A Guide to the Gods, Heroes, Rituals, and Beliefs*, Oxford: Oxford University Press.

Lokasenna = Jónas Kristjánsson, Vésteinn Ólason and Þórður Ingi Guðjónsson (eds.) (2014). *Eddukvæði*, 2 vols, Reykjavík: Hið íslenzka fornritafélag.

Marold, E. (2017). 'Úlfr Uggason, *Húsdrápa* 3' in Gade, K. E. and Marold, E. (eds.), *Skaldic Poetry of the Scandinavian Middle Ages* 3, *Poetry from Treatises on Poetics*, 2 vol, Turnhout: Brepols, pp. 412-413.

Meletinskij, E. M. (1973). 'Scandinavian Mythology as a System (Part 1)', *Journal of Symbolic Anthropology*, 1, pp. 43-57.

Meletinskij, E. M. (1977). 'Scandinavian Mythology as a System of Oppositions', in Jason, H. and Segal, D. (eds.), *Patterns in Oral Literature*, The Hague: Mouton Publishers, pp. 251-260.

Rösli, L. (2015). *Topographien der eddischen Mythen: Eine Untersuchung zu den Raumnarrativen und den narrativen Räumen in der Lieder-Edda und der Prosa-Edda*. Tübingen: A. Francke Verlag.

Rösli, L. (2017). 'The Myth of Útgarðr – A Toponym as a Basis for an Old Norse System of Values?', *Viking and Medieval Scandinavia*, 13, pp. 211-227.

Schjødt, J. P. (1990). 'Horizontale und vertikale Achsen in der vorchristlichen skandinavischen Kosmologie', *Scripta Instituti Donneriani Aboensis*, 13, pp. 35-57.

Simek, R. (1993). *Dictionary of Northern Mythology*, trans. by Hall, A., Cambridge: D. S. Brewer.

Skáldskaparmál = Faulkes, A. (ed.) 1998. *Snorri Sturluson, Edda. Skáldskaparmál*, 2 vols, Exeter: Viking Society for Northern Research.

SkP = Gade, K. E. and Marold, E. (eds.) (2017). *Skaldic Poetry of the Scandinavian Middle Ages* 3, *Poetry from Treatises on Poetics*, 2 vol, Turnhout: Brepols.

Steinsland, G. (2005). 'The Late Iron Age Worldview and the Concept of "Utmark"', in Holm, I., Innselset, S. M., and Øye, I. (eds.), *'Utmark': The Outfield as Industry and Ideology in the Iron Age and the Middle Ages*, Bergen: University of Bergen, pp. 137-146.

Vǫluspá = Jónas Kristjánsson, Vésteinn Ólason and Þórður Ingi Guðjónsson (eds.) (2014). *Eddukvæði*, 2 vols, Reykjavík: Hið íslenzka fornritafélag.

Wanner, K. J. (2008). *Snorri Sturluson and the Edda. The Conversion of Cultural Capital in Medieval Scandinavia*. Toronto: University of Toronto Press.

Þrymskviða = Jónas Kristjánsson, Vésteinn Ólason and Þórður Ingi Guðjónsson (eds.) (2014). *Eddukvæði*, 2 vols, Reykjavík: Hið íslenzka fornritafélag.

A Haunted Home on a Northern Moor in Selma Lagerlöf's *Stenkumlet*

Victoria Ralph

Introduction

Stenkumlet (The Cairn of Stones) is one of three Old Norse-influenced, quite under-studied short stories including *De fågelfrie* and *Reors saga* in the short story collection *Osynliga länkar* (1897) by Swedish author Selma Lagerlöf (1858-1940).[1] The stories are all set in medieval times and reflect the confrontation of Old Norse heathendom and Christianity in a transition period not long after the Christianisation of Norway by King Óláfr *helgi* Haraldsson, known as St Olav (ruled ca. 1015-1028). Although the exact historical setting is not specified in *Stenkumlet*, Lagerroth underlines that Lagerlöf regarded *Stenkumlet* as a companion piece to *De fågelfrie* in time and milieu (Lagerroth 1963: 203, 332). Graves points out that the time period and location of *De fågelfrie* is indicated in a passing reference to 'Viken – the Oslo Fjord some time but not too long after St Olav had Christianised the area, that is after about 1030' (Graves 1994: 54). Similarly, Reor, the chief protagonist in *Reors saga*, is described as being baptised when St Olav rooted out the old belief (Lagerlöf 1897: 121).

Stenkumlet merges motifs from revenant stories in the medieval Icelandic sagas with the two most outstanding geographical features of Swedish Bohuslän – the heather moor and ancient stone monuments.[2] These features are re-arranged to mirror the ghostly landscape setting of the saga revenant stories through placing the grave-mound of King Atli from the Old Norse *Vǫlsunga saga* (*The Saga of the Volsungs*) in front of the home of Swedish peasants. *Vǫlsunga saga* was written down by an anonymous author in thirteenth-century Iceland and is classified as a legendary saga.[3] In an era of nineteenth-century national romanticism, *Vǫlsunga saga* with the famous stories about the Volsungs, Gjukings and Budlungs and a cast of remarkable characters such as Sigurðr *fáfnisbani* and the legendary Valkyrie Brynhildr was well-known, widely translated and popularised through Wagner's opera *The Ring of the Nibelung* (first complete performance 1876). Medieval Icelandic sagas were widely translated and used as part of the construction of national identities (see Wawn 2000: 328-337). Scandinavian translations of *The Saga of the Volsungs* are included in Horn's 1876 Danish translation of the prose version entitled *Saga om Vølsungerne* in *Nordiske heltesagœr* and Gödecke's 1877 Swedish translation of the poetic sources in *Edda: en Isländsk Samling Folkliga Forntidsdikter om Nordens Gudar och Hjältar*.

In *Stenkumlet* the saga motif of the ghostly cairn is combined with local legends about King Dårskild and a dancing bride who was spirited away into a mountain and petrified into stone at Bruda-Bärget. Lagerroth suggests that the folklore stories Lagerlöf used as source texts were published in Oedeman's *Chorographia Bohusiensis* (1746: 363), Holmberg's *Bohusläns historia* II (1867: 32) and Afzelius's *Sago-häfder* IV (1845: 170) (Lagerroth: 1963: 204-206, 332). Lagerlöf's new, Victorian-styled ghost story thus combines the old and modern genres with the new, up-to-date psychological realism.[4] Moreover, it transforms the natural Bohuslän features of the heather and stone into Gothic symbolism from Victorian and Romantic literature – the heathland with a Gothic ring of wilderness and the cairn of stones as 'den götiska symbolen' (Mjöberg 1968: 428) (the Gothic symbol).[5] Wijkmark's analysis (2014) of Lagerlöf's short story *Gammal fäbodsägen* (An Old Tale from the Mountains), a narrative of a murder in a mountain-hut that was published in 1914, demonstrates that 'elements of uncanniness create psychological depth'. She pinpoints 'the uncanny as a special variant of horror that can be regarded as a 'central element in Lagerlöf's *œuvre*', and describes her as a prominent representative of 'the Gothic boom in Swedish literature at the turn of the twentieth century'. Furthermore, Wijkmark defines the 'Gothic as a genre, dealing with the experience of reality expressed by the concept of the uncanny' (Wijkmark 2014: 232-244). *Stenkumlet* relates the spooky events that occur in the haunted home of Swedish peasants on a remote northern moor in the region of Bohuslän on the border of Sweden and Norway.

Wijkmark defines the primary aspects of 'the uncanny' as 'insecurity' and 'ambiguity' and connects them to fantastic literature. In her analysis of the genre mix in *Gammal fäbodsägen* she explains that '[t]he mixing of genres can be placed in the context of the shift taking place in fantastic literature in the nineteenth century' (Wijkmark 2014: 234, 239). According to Jackson, this may be 'the juncture when readings of otherness as supernatural [...] were being slowly replaced and disturbed by readings of otherness as natural and subjectively generated' (Jackson 1981: 62).

In the following, I will introduce the theory of 'the uncanny' to the *Stenkumlet* studies, as well as some new ideas on conceptual connections to writings of Freud, inspired by Wijkmark (2014). My main argument is that 'the uncanny' elements in *Stenkumlet* show that it cannot be read as a tale of the supernatural only. Furthermore, I will try to show that a reading of *Stenkumlet* influenced by 'the uncanny' reveals a number of feminist and pacifist themes.

Stenkumlet is of particular interest because it is the first of Lagerlöf's Old Norse-inspired works in which she uses the heathen/Christian conflict in the Old Norse sources to tell another story that is linked to her pacifism.[6] My research concentrates on Lagerlöf's Old Norse works set in medieval Kungahälla (Old

Norse *Konungahella*) when Bohuslän was part of Ranrike (Old Norse Ránríki) in the eastern part of Norwegian Viken. The anti-war poem *Kungahällas fall* (1894; *The Fall of Kungahälla*) and the short story collection *Drottningar i Kungahälla* (1899; *The Queens of Kungahälla*) arise from 'the exploration of local and national history, mythology and folklore' that were an integral part of the nineteenth-century national consciousness-raising process discussed by Wawn (2000: 330). However, the Kungahälla works also fit into Wawn's category of writers 'though proudly aware of their country's medieval heritage, felt little nostalgia for Viking brutalities' (Wawn 2000: 331).[7]

Content

The story tells of a couple who meet on the heath who are descendants of slaves who had fled to the forest. Tönne watches Jofrid dancing between ancient stone cairns on the heather moor. Under the largest pile of stones lies Old King Atle surrounded by the grave mounds of his warriors who fell in a battle. Jofrid's husband Tönne builds a home for her opposite Atle's cairn with a heather roof and stone threshold. When Jofrid crosses the doorstep of her new home for the first time she sees the pile of stones transform into the figure of an ancient warrior. The childless married couple foster the baby son of a peasant in the valley whose wife has died. But Tönne and Jofrid do not care for their foster-son properly and he dies in infancy. After the dead child returns to haunt them, Tönne wants to confess their neglect of him, do penance and offer compensation to the child's father by giving him all their possessions and themselves as slaves. But Jofrid doesn't want to lose her freedom and home comforts. Unable to find any peace of mind, she sits on the stone doorstep and her second vision of Atle is turned into a spectral prop to ignore the voice of her conscience and reject Christian repentance. Her final vision of the old stone warrior is a premonition of her death.

Whereas the hauntings of the saga revenants impart supernatural or religious explanations, the apparitions in Lagerlöf's ghost story can be given psychological interpretations. The approaches I will take include an examination of Lagerlöf's use of Old Norse sources to put forward a modern subjective text. To illustrate, the image of the *draugr* (revenant) is updated by Lagerlöf who employs her 'cairn-dweller' to typify a 'fighting spirit'. I utilise Royle's definition of the three characteristics of 'the uncanny' as it is depicted in literature (Royle 2003), in conjunction with Freud's concepts of *Heimlich/Unheimlich* in his 1919 essay *Das Unheimliche* (*The Uncanny*) to analyse the concept of the haunted home as an uncanny home in a heathen setting (Freud 1995). My overall reading uses Freudian insights to show that Atle's ghost is not a supernatural manifestation but 'the uncanny' effect of Jofrid projecting her unconscious desires and fears onto the environment. For example, the pile of stones is uncannily animated into the image of Atle, the old stone warrior who transforms into Jofrid's spokesman for heathen hard-heartedness, indifference and fatalism in the battle with her conscience over the child's death.

Lagerlöf uses the heathen/Christian conflict in the Old Norse sources to question how pacifism and Christianity fit in with Viking violence exploring themes of retribution or redemption. She re-tells Kungahälla's warring past from the perspectives of women characters in *Heimskringla*,[8] a famous collection of Old Norse Kings' sagas written around 1230 by the Icelandic saga-writer and politician Snorri Sturluson (1179-1241). As a pacifist and activist in the struggle for women's suffrage,[9] Lagerlöf was critical of *Heimskringla* as an example of traditional male history that focused on wars and political events only. Apart from a small number of powerful queens, few women are mentioned in Snorri's history except in subordinate roles. By contrast, Lagerroth states that Lagerlöf's aim in *Drottningar i Kungahälla* was 'att skriva om den tid och de tilldragelser Snorre berättar om, men inte från männens synvinkel utan från *kvinnornas*' (Lagerroth 1963: 92, emphasis original) (to write about the period and the events Snorri narrates about, not from the perspective of the men but from that of the *women*) (English translation my own). Stenberg emphasises that '[f]or a long time, her intention was to write women into history, a project which later became *Drottningar i Kungahälla*' (Stenberg 2014: 31). Lagerlöf's Kungahälla works pre-date her major pacifist novel *Bannlyst* (*Banished*) that was published at the end of the First World War in 1918 and is also located in Bohuslän where she witnessed the aftermath of the Battle of Jutland as countless corpses of dead soldiers floated in from the sea.[10]

Saga revenants

In *The Idea of North*, Davidson traces the origins of a northern revenant tradition back to medieval Iceland where 'the ghost stories in the sagas are mostly set in the period immediately after the conversion of the island to Christianity' (Davidson 2005: 145). Lindow follows a Scandinavian folklore tradition of the living dead that extends as far back as there are written records, to the terrifying *draugr* revenants in the sagas and identifies the most famous *draugr* as Glámr from the medieval Icelandic *Grettis saga* (Lindow 1978: 15).[11] Significantly, Lagerroth refers to Lagerlöf's knowledge of Danish translations of the same saga by Thordarson and Winkel Horn from 1859 to 1874 (Lagerroth 1963: 187, 206, 331).

Set in the years immediately following the Christianisation of Iceland in 999-1000, *Grettis saga* reflects the juxtaposition of heathen and Christian values and beliefs and demonstrates Davidson's theory that the coexistence of parallel belief systems provided 'the mainspring of the ancient Scandinavian ghost narratives' (Davidson 2005: 150). The saga narrates, among others, the wrestling matches of the Christian outlaw-hero Grettir with heathen revenants who are portrayed not as wispy spectres but as the strong, corporeal living dead (see Guðni Jónsson 1936, pp. 56-61, 107-123). In Chapter 18, Grettir breaks into the *haugr* (sepulchral mound) of Kárr inn gamli (Kar the Old), a revenant characterised as *haug-búi* (mound-dweller). Grettir fights and kills the revenant and takes his treasure. Chapters 32-35, then, narrate a series of terrifying Christmas hauntings at the farmer Þórhallr's farm in Iceland. Þórhallr hires a shepherd from Sweden called Glámr – a heathen and foreign outsider. Glámr refuses to follow the Christian custom of fasting on Christmas Eve and disappears in a fierce snowstorm. On Christmas Day a search-party discover his blackened and swollen body in a mountain valley. Attempts to move the body of Glámr to church fail and he is buried under a *dys* (cairn of stones). Glámr returns from the dead to haunt before he is eventually killed by Grettir for a second-time and the revenant's cremated ashes are buried in a skin bag in the wilderness, far away from people.

Lagerlöf's familiarity with Danish translations of *Grettis saga* may have inspired her to re-map the saga motif of the revenant's cairn opposite the rustic home out in the wilds of a Bohuslän heath. The saga revenant stories can be seen to haunt or inhabit Lagerlöf's text as the localised place name of *Dårskilds högar* (stone circle formations where a legendary king is buried surrounded by his men) is changed to 'kung Atles hög' (King Atle's mound) (Lagerlöf 1897: 100: English translation my own). Lagerroth states that the name Dårskild was used in the first published version of *Stenkumlet* in the Swedish journal *Dagny* in 1893 but was eventually changed to Atle in *Osynliga länkar* (1897). He connects the name Atle to heathen kings in Swedish chronicles and to Attila the Hun in *Vǫlsunga saga*. (Lagerroth 1963: 206, 332). Lagerroth emphasises that the name Atle has 'en särskilt fornnordisk klang' (a distinct Old Norse ring to it) (Lagerroth 1963: 206; English translation my own) that characterises heathen hardness. His conclusion carries a ring of truth when we consider that it an important part of Lagerlöf's pacifist narrative strategy to create not a local but a more universally recognisable Old Norse male archetypal figure of war in the character of Atli, the ruthless warrior king in *Vǫlsunga saga*.

Uncanny home / uncanny ghosts

In Chapter 9 of *The Uncanny*, Royle discusses Moberley's story *Inexplicable* (1917) with reference to Freud's previously mentioned essay *Das Unheimliche*, and defines three characteristics of 'the uncanny as it is depicted in literature'. Firstly, 'it is a story about a house, and more particularly a new "home", and it begins at the threshold, with a complexity and uncertainty of crossing a threshold, with an experience of liminality (the word comes from the Latin "limen", threshold)' (Royle 2003: 136). Secondly, it foregrounds a sense of the familiar or 'ordinary'. Finally, the text is self-reflexive, aware of its own fictionality and participation in a tradition of supernatural, gothic or uncanny fiction.

Royle's three literary characteristics are relevant to an analysis of the uncanniness of the haunted home on the northern moor in *Stenkumlet*. For example, the complexity and uncertainty of crossing the threshold are due to Jofrid's doubts about marrying a weak and dull man with a poor livelihood that are foreshadowed in the text before she steps over the door-sill of the new home for the first time. Although she was drawn to Tönne's good heart, nevertheless '[h]on ville hafva en stark och frisk man' (Lagerlöf 1897: 99) ([s]he wished to have a strong and healthy husband) (Flach 1899: 78). At sunset Jofrid opens the door and 'Kungahögen låg midt för dörren, och bakom den såg hon just solen sjunka' (Lagerlöf 1897: 102) ([t]he king's grave lay opposite the door and behind it she saw the sun setting) (Flach 1899: 81). As the sun sets low Jofrid sees the pile of stones animated into the figure of Atle as a mighty old warrior. The scene of everyday domestic bliss as she happily hangs up her weavings is upset by a liminal experience. Here, as in so many other parts of the text, Lagerlöf's use of Swedish *hög* (mound) as an alternative to *kummel* (cairn) is an allusion to Gothic fiction, to what Mjöberg describes as 'den gamla götiska klichén "ättehögen"' (Mjöberg 1967-1968: 429, 164) (the old gothic cliché 'the sepulchral mound') (English translation my own).

Freud's concept of *Heimlich/Unheimlich* is also applicable to illustrate the unsettling effects of 'the uncanny' in the haunted home as follows (summarised from Jackson 1981: 65):

> *Das Heimliche* has two levels of meaning: 1) It signifies that which is homely and familiar. 2) It also means that which is concealed from others: all that is hidden, secreted, occluded.

> *Das Unheimliche* means that which is un-homely, unfamiliar or strange and functions to dis-cover, reveal, expose areas normally kept out of sight.

The home that Tönne built for Jofrid on the heath is cosy and homely: 'Så snart Jofrid hade kommit öfver tröskeln, kände hon ett hems glada trefnad omge henne' (Lagerlöf 1897: 101) (As soon as Jofrid had crossed the threshold, she felt the pleasant cosiness of home surrounding her) (Flach 1899: 80). But *Das Heimliche* of the familiar home of Swedish peasants turns into *Das Unheimliche* of an unfamiliar frightening place when their foster-son dies and haunts the stone threshold.

The construction of domal space underlines Royle's description that 'the uncanny' 'disturbs any straightforward sense of what is inside and what is outside. The uncanny has to do with a strangeness of frames and borders, an experience of liminality' (Royle 2003: 2). The heather heath is conceptualised as heathen and the uncanny home is infiltrated by the outer landscape features of the heather and stone that permeate the inner structure. To exemplify, the uneven floorboards where the heather grew and blossomed underneath 'stack upp förvägna röda klasar genom springorna' (Lagerlöf 1897: 100) (pushed up bold red clusters through the cracks) (Flach 1899: 79). The stone threshold is situated in the gap between walls, neither inside nor outside the building and acts as a sort of gateway. Jofrid is is no shrinking violet and is likened to the heather: 'Andra unga tärnor likna rosor och liljor, men hon var som ljungen, stark, munter och lysande' (Lagerlöf 1897: 94) (Other young maidens resemble roses and lilies, but she was like the heather, strong, gay and glowing) (Flach: 1899: 74). Her heather-like characteristics are reflected in her appearance and in the home, and extend to the moor outside and act on the stone element in Atle, the image of a warrior and old stone-cold heathenism. Jofrid and Atle appear to be part of the natural landscape setting and are coloured by it. Her face is red as heather and his face is as grey as stone. The redness of the heather can also be linked to Jofrid's warring mentality as signified by her bright red face and the heather heath can be interpreted as a battlefield suffused with bloodshed where Atle 'hade neglagt högtals med fiender där på ljungfältet, och vadat fram i blodströmmar, som hade forsat mellan tufvorna' (Lagerlöf 1897: 109) (had overthrown hundreds of enemies there on the heath and waded through the streams of blood that had poured between the clumps) (Flach 1899: 87).

Wijkmark explains that 'Freud emphasises insecurity related to the supernatural as an example of the uncanny' (2014: 234). Freud's ideas can be applied to the new textual surrounding of *Stenkumlet* because of the ambiguity in the text that is open to double-meanings. The reader can never be quite sure if the pile of stones that turn into Jofrid's visions of Atle are supernatural apparitions or her psychological projections onto the environment. But a rational interpretation of events shows that Jofrid is haunted by her worries and obsessions, for the ghostly sightings of Atle occur during her psychological crises, always in dim lighting, at sunset or in moonlight. Atle's first appearance occurs during a betrothal dilemma when Jofrid enters her new home for the first time and sees the pile of stones transmute into 'den gamle kung Atle själf' (Lagerlöf 1897: 103) (old King Atle himself) (Flach: 1899: 82) who is represented as a living being '[o]ch han lefde, denne stenman. Han log och blinkade mot henne' (Lagerlöf 1897: 103) ([a]nd he was alive, that man of stone. He smiled and winked at her) (Flach: 1899: 82) Atle's ghost can be interpreted as Jofrid's fantasy man, her suppressed longings for a physically strong husband instead of her feeble spouse who is described as 'gulblek, köttlös och blodfattig' (Lagerlöf 1897: 96) (pallid, thin and anaemic) (Flach 1899: 75).

Jofrid's major crisis is the domestic conflict with her husband that follows the death of their foster-child. Her anxiety begins at the funeral where she realises that she is different to the other women from the valley who talk continually about their children because her nurturing is directed at making a man out of Tönne: 'Kvinnor bruka hafva sin stora lust och glädje af att handskas med barn, men Jofrid hade en man, för hvilken hon i mycket måste bära en mors omsorg' (Lagerlöf 1897: 106) (Women usually enjoy nothing better than to take care of a child; but Jofrid had a husband, whom she often had to care for like a mother) (Flach 1899: 84).

Refusing to take responsibility for the child's death, she has a second vision of the old stone warrior as she takes refuge in heathen fatalism and hears the whispers of old stone-cold heathenism from her mouthpiece Atle: 'Hvarför ångra? Gudarna äro de, som styra. Nornorna spinna lifvets tråd' (Lagerlöf 1897: 109) (Why repent? The gods rule us. The fates spin the threads of life) (Flach 1899: 87).[12] Jofrid's final vision of Atle is a premonition of her death. She receives her death blow when she gets caught up in the violent frenzy of the dancing out on the heath, and is thrown against the stones of the king's cairn and dies.

Stenkumlet also contains four of the thirteen unlucky forms suggested by literary theorists Bennett and Royle in *The Uncanny* as repetition, animism, death and ghosts (Bennett & Royle 2009: 36-40). Their concept of uncanny repetition includes the experience of *déjà-vu* that is pertinent to the sense of Jofrid´s death as a re-enactment of one of Lagerlöf's source texts, the legend of the dancing bride petrified into stone at Bruda-Bärget. There is an uncanny sense of *déjà-vu*; as Jofrid's limbs become heavier and more stone-like she also becomes more troll-like. 'Det förekom henne, som om hon vore af sten, ett tungt stenbeläte liksom gamle kung Atle' (Lagerlöf 1897: 114-115) (It seemed to her as if she were of stone, a heavy stone image like old King Atle) (Flach 1899: 92). A supernatural folkloristic explanation of events could be that she became a troll herself who turned into stone. But the troll-likeness in Jofrid contains more nineteenth-century psychological depth and is linked to Lagerroth's insights into her heather-likeness in the text: 'Men såsom ljungen kan förvandlas till en mantel för kung Atle, så kan det ljunglika i Jofrids sinne bemantla hjärtlöshet och egoism, njutningslust och präktbegär' (Lagerroth 1963: 210) (As the heather can change into a mantle for King Atle, so can the heather likeness in Jofrid's nature cover heartlesness, egoism, lust for pleasure and desire for splendour) (English translation my own). The psychological realism in the form of her thoughts indicates self-awareness that she knew to the last 'att hon ej hade kunnat besegra stenkonungen i sitt eget hjärta, som Atle blef henne öfvermäktig' (Lagerlöf 1897: 118) (that it was because she had not been able to conquer the stone king in her own heart that Atle had power over her) (Flach 1899: 95).

Conclusion

Lagerlöf reverses and questions essentialist culturally constructed gender oppositions in her representation of Jofrid as a heathen warlike woman. There are echoes in her characterisation of Brynhildr in *Vǫlsunga saga* who was also skilled in handicrafts. Jofrid resembles a Brynhildian type whose deep structure is discussed by Heinrichs in 'Annat er várt eðli: the type of the prepatriarchal woman in Old Norse literature' and whose traits show in the characterisation of Sigríðr *stórráða* (Heinrichs 1986: 110-140). *Stenkumlet* is especially interesting in Lagerlöf's Old Norse inspired *œuvre* as a forerunner to her more in-depth study of two female archetypes or stereotypes from Old Norse Literature in *Sigrid Storråda* in *Drottningar i Kungahälla*. In this later short story Lagerlöf's Sigrid Storråda (a Valkyrie) is modelled on her mighty namesake Sigríðr in stórráða in *Óláfs saga Tryggvasonar* in *Heimskringla* and is recognised by her character of King Óláfr as Brunhildr (Ralph 2017: 190-191).

Tjeder, Sundevall and Persson discuss the dichotomy of 'peace-loving women and war-prone' men as a historical construct and the concept of the 'feminisation of peace' in nineteenth-century Sweden (Tjeder, Sundevall and Persson 2014: 40). The image of Jofrid as a warring woman lacking maternal instincts contradicts nineteenth-century Swedish feminist and pacifist ideals rooted in Christian beliefs and influenced by difference feminism. For example, the influential Ellen Key regarded motherhood as 'women's highest cultural task' with 'the potential to transform the world' (Forsås-Scott 1997: 30). Contemporary feminist/pacifist discourse did not confine to the home the role of women as natural peacemakers (based on their traditional role as mothers). Emilia Broomé, who founded Sweden's first women-only peace organisation in 1898, *Sveriges kvinnliga fredsförening* (Sweden's women's peace association), also exhorted women to join peace organisations and to agitate for peace outside of their homes (Tjeder, Sundevall and Persson 2014: 50).

Lagerlöf's own feminist/pacifist vision in *Stenkumlet* protests against militarism but emphasises human, caring values instead of maternal instincts and is based on the imagery of the heart as a place of compassion and love. The old king is seen sitting deep in the human heart: 'Han var den store stenkämpen, som såg nöd och armod vandra förbi, utan att hans stenhjärta rördes'

(Lagerlöf 1897: 115) (He was the great stone warrior who saw famine and poverty pass by without his stone heart being moved) (Flach 1899: 92). Jofrid, therefore, is not actually condemned by the author for her inadequacies as a mother but her violent death is portrayed as retribution for her hard-heartedness.

Endnotes

[1] Not much research has been done on the three texts. Only Lagerlöf specialist Lagerroth has done studies on all three (Lagerroth 1963: 186-251). Otherwise, Mjöberg has concentrated on *De fågelfrie* and *Stenkumlet* in his monograph on the post-medieval reception of Old Norse literature (Mjöberg 1967-8: 425-424, 430). Finally, Graves has analysed *De fågelfrie* (Graves 1994: 51-61). All three scholars have mainly focused on the heathen/ Christian conflict and themes of retribution in the texts. The short stories were translated by Flach as *The Outlaws*, *The King's Grave* and *The Saga of Reor* in *Invisible Links* (Flach 1899). For *Stenkumlet*, I have used my more literal translation of the title as *The Cairn of Stones*. All other English translations quoted are taken from Flach's *The King's Grave* unless otherwise indicated.

[2] Medieval Icelandic sagas were written down by anonymous authors in the thirteenth and fourteenth centuries and mainly narrate events set in the so-called Saga Age of Iceland (930-1030). Saga revenant stories are not a specific genre but are parts of the greater *Íslendingasögur* corpus and appear in selected sagas such as *Grettis saga* and *Eyrbyggja saga*. In the introduction to *Three Icelandic Outlaw Sagas*, Anthony Faulkes discusses some episodes with supernatural elements in the outlaw sagas that derive from Scandinavian folk-tales whereas others are more literary in conception (Faulkes 2004: xxiv-xxv).

[3] *Vǫlsunga saga* is based on Old Norse heroic poetry recorded in the thirteenth-century *Poetic Edda* narrating popular mythic-legendary history from Northern Europe in the Migration Period (375-583 AD). For the historical and literary-historical background to *Vǫlsunga saga*, see Grimstad (2000: 13-75).

[4] The Victorian period covers the reign of the British Queen Victoria 1837-1901. Ghost stories are a special category of the fantastic evolving from folklore and developing through Gothic horror fiction to become widely popularised in the Victorian period (Jackson 1981: 68). For the Victorian ghost story tradition, see Davidson (2005: 150-158).

[5] Heathlands form familiar topography in Gothic fiction and Victorian and Romantic literature. For a summary, see Cuddon (2011: 356).

[6] For further research on the subject, see my MPhil thesis 'Lagerlöf's Old Norse *Kungahälla*: Perspectives of Women and Pacifism', which is expected to be submitted in 2022.

[7] During the Viking Age (793-1068) shipborne heathen warriors from Scandinavia raided, traded and settled many parts of Europe. For the popular image of the Vikings, see Boyer (1994: 69-81).

[8] Lagerlöf made use of Munch's 1859 Norwegian translation of *Heimskringla* (Lagerroth 1963: 49, 88, 126, 298, 323, 326), as well as Hildebrand's Swedish translation from 1889 (Ralph 2017: 191).

[9] An example of Lagerlöf's activity in the struggle for women's suffrage is that she became a member of the suffrage committee in her hometown of Falun in 1905. Furthermore, in 1911, she gave a speech named 'Hem och stat' (Home and state) at the International Congress for Women's Suffrage in Stockholm.

[10] The setting is important because Bohuslän was the site of border wars for centuries until it was finally ceded to Sweden in 1658 by the Peace of Roskilde. Thomsen explains that '[o]ne of the primary sources of inspiration for *Bannlyst* was the author's personal experience of the gruesome effects of the Battle of Jutland between Britain and Germany on 31 May-1 June 1916, the largest naval battle of the First World War, while holidaying with Elkan in Strömstad on the Bohuslän coast' (Thomsen 2012: 13, see also 12-17 for 'the uncanny' in *Bannlyst*).

[11] Grettir is the chief protagonist of *Grettis saga* (which was written down anonymously in Iceland in 1310-1320). The saga is generally categorised as an Outlaw saga (a sub-genre of the *Íslendingasögur*) which partly deals with the phenomenon of *draugr*.

[12] Flach translates 'Nornorna' as 'the fates' interpreting the attributes of the triad of women called Urd, Verðandi and Skuld (Past, Present and Future) as women of destiny in Nordic mythology. Simek explains that the spinning or weaving of fate could be influenced by classical mythology. The poem *Darraðarljóð* in *Njáls saga* mixes the characteristics of the norns with Valkyries who metaphorically depict the battle in their weaving (Simek 1993: 236-237).

References

Afzelius, A. A. (1844-1868). *Swenska folkets sago-häfder,* Vol 1-11, Stockholm: Hæggström.

Bennett, A. and Royle, N. (2009). 'The uncanny', in Bennett, A. and Royle, N. (eds.): *An Introduction to Literature, Criticism and Theory.* 4th Edition. Harlow: Pearson Longman, pp. 35-43.

Boyer, R., (1994). 'Vikings, Sagas and Wasa Bread' in Wawn, A. (ed.): *Northern antiquity: the post-medieval reception of Edda and saga.* Enfield Lock Middlesex: Hisarlik Press, pp. 69-81.

Cuddon, J. A. (2011). *The Penguin Dictionary Of Literary Terms And Literary Theory.* Fourth Edition. London: Penguin Books.

Davidson, P. (2005). *The Idea of North.* London: Reaktion Books.

Faulkes, A. (trans.). (2004). *Three Icelandic Outlaw Sagas.* London: Viking Society for Northern Research.

Flach, P. B. (trans.) (1899). 'The King's Grave', in: Lagerlöf, S.: *Invisible Links.* Boston: Little Brown, pp. 71-95.

Forsås-Scott, H. (1997). *Swedish Women's Writing 1850-1995.* London and Atlantic Highlands, NJ: The Athlone Press.

Freud, S. (1995) [1919]. 'The Uncanny', in Freud, S.: *The Standard Edition of the Complete Psychological Works of Sigmund Freud*, XVIII: *1917-1919, An Infantile Neurosis and Other Works.* Trans. J. Strachey. London: Hogarth Press, pp. 217-253.

Graves, P. (1994). 'Selma Lagerlöf's "De fågelfrie": The Divide between the Seen and the Spoken', in Death, S. and Forsås-Scott, H. (eds.): *A Century of Swedish Narrative: Essays in Honour of Karin Petherick.* London: Norvik Press, pp. 51-61.

Grimstad, K. (trans.) (2000). *Vǫlsunga saga: The Saga of the Volsungs.* Saarbrücken: AQ-Verlag.

Guðni Jónsson (ed.). (1936). *Grettis saga Ásmundarsonar.* Íslenzk fornrit 7. Reykjavík: Hið íslenzka fornritafélag.

Gödecke, P. A. (trans.). (1877). *Edda: en Isländsk Samling Folkliga Forntidsdikter om Nordens Gudar och Hjältar.* (1877). Stockholm: P. A. Norstedt & Söner.

Heinrichs, A. (1986). 'Annat er várt eðli: the type of the prepatriarchal woman in Old Norse literature' in Lindow, J., Lönnroth, L. and Weber, G. W.(eds.): *Structure and Meaning in Old Norse Literature: New Approaches to Textual Analysis and Literary Criticism*, Odense: Odense University Press, pp. 110-140.

Holmberg, A. E. (1867). *Bohusläns historia och beskrivning af Axel Emanuel Holmberg efter författerens död genomsedd och rättad af G.Brusewitz*. Örebro: Lindh.

Horn, W. (trans.) (1874). *Grette Asmundssons Saga*. Copenhagen: C.A. Reitzels Forlag.

Horn, W. (trans.) (1876). *Saga om Vølsungerne* in *Nordiske heltesagœr*. Copenhagen: Samfundet til den danske literaturs fremme.

Jackson, R. (1981). *Fantasy: The Literature of Subversion*, London: Methuen & Co Ltd.

Lagerlöf, S. (1897). *Osynliga länkar*. Stockholm: Bonnier.

Lagerroth, E. (1963). 'Stenkumlet' in, Lagerroth, E.: *Selma Lagerlöf Och Bohuslän, En studie i hennes 90-talsdiktning*, Lund: Gleerups Förlag, pp. 203-213.

Lindow, J. (1978). *Swedish Legends and Folktales*. Berkeley: Univ. of California Press.

Mjöberg, J. (1967-1968). *Drömmen om sagatiden*. Stockholm: Berlingska Boktryckeriet.

Oedeman, J. (1746). *Chorographia Bohusiensis*, Stockholm: hos Lars Salvius på egen konstnad.

Ralph, Victoria, (2017). 'Old Norse Dreamscapes And Seascapes of War: *Sigrid Storråda* (Valkyrie) by Selma Lagerlöf' in Jennings, A., Reeploeg, S. and Watt, A. (eds.): *Northern Atlantic Islands And The Sea: Seascapes and Dreamscapes*. Newcastle upon Tyne: Cambridge Scholars Publishing, pp. 180-194.

Royle, N. (2003). *The Uncanny*, Manchester: Manchester University Press.

Simek, R. (1993). *Dictionary of Norse Mythology*. Cambridge: D. S. Brewer.

Stenberg, L. (2014). 'A Star In A Constellation: The international women's movement as a context for reading the works of Selma Lagerlöf', in Forsås-Scott, H., Stenberg, L. and Thomsen, B. T. (eds.): *Re-Mapping Lagerlöf: Performance, Intermediality, and European Transmissions.* Lund: Nordic Academic Press, pp. 24-38.

Thomsen. B. T. (2012). '(Trans)national Geographies and Alternative Families in Selma Lagerlöf's Bannlyst', *European Journal of Scandinavian Studies,* 42 (1), pp. 1-18.

Thordarson, G. (trans.) (1859). *Grettis saga ved G. Magnússon og G. Thordarson.* Copenhagen: Berlingske bogtrykkeri ved N H Stenderup.

Tjeder, D., Sundevall, F and Persson, A. (2014). 'Gendering Peace, 1850-2000: A Framework of Analysis' in Ahlbäck, A. and Sundevall, F. (eds.): *Gender, War and Peace: Breaking up the Borderlines.* Joensuu: UPEF, pp. 40-59.

Wawn, A. (2000). 'The Post-Medieval Reception of Old Norse and Old Icelandic Literature', in McTurk, R. (ed.): *A Companion to Old-Norse Icelandic Literature and Culture.* Oxford: Blackwell Publishing, pp. 320-337.

Wijkmark, S. (2014). 'Violence and the uncanny', in Forsås-Scott, H., Stenberg, L. and Thomsen, B. (eds.): *Re-mapping Lagerlöf: Performance, Intermediality, and European Transmissions.* Lund Sweden: Nordic Academic Press, pp. 232-244.

Notes on contributors:

Christian Cooijmans is a British Academy Research Fellow at the University of Liverpool. Having obtained his doctorate from the University of Edinburgh, his research focusses on the reach and repercussions of viking endeavour across mainland Europe, as well as its ensuing, premodern historiography.

Dr Jan D. Cox: BA (Hons) Oxford Brookes, MA Bristol, PhD Leeds. His thesis examined the reception of Nordic art in Europe 1878-1889. Publications include book chapters on the Battle of Kringen (1612), and Vilhelm Hammershøi's pictures at the 1889 Exposition Universelle. In 2017, he was the major catalogue contributor to "Romanticism in the North - from Friedrich to Turner" (Groninger Museum).

Andrea Freund BA (Hons) University of Nottingham, MLitt from the University of the Highlands and Islands, currently PhD candidate at the same institution. She has research interests in Runology and Old Norse philology in an interdisciplinary perspective, focusing on the Viking Age and Late Norse period in the North Atlantic. Andrea is currently employed at the Department of Linguistics and Scandinavian Studies, University of Oslo, teaching Runology and Old Norse.

Isabelle Gapp completed a PhD in History of Art at the University of York in 2019. Her thesis was titled, *A Circumpolar Landscape: Art and Environment in Scandinavia and North America, 1896-1933.* Isabelle's research looks at questions of ecology and gender in the landscape painting of the Circumpolar North during the 19th and early 20th century.

Blake Middleton, PhD candidate, University of Aberdeen, Centre for Scandinavian Studies. PhD thesis analyses the semantic development and narrative use of the *jǫtnar* (giants) in both the *Poetic Edda* and *Snorra Edda*. Research Interests: Old Norse mythology, Old Norse *jǫtnar*, medieval narrative literature, adaptation of medieval narrative literature and mythology in modern popular-culture and visual media (TV, Film, Theatre, etc.).

Victoria Lesley Ralph is an MPhil student at the Scandinavian Studies Department, University College London. The title of her thesis is 'Lagerlöf's Old Norse Kungahälla: Perspectives of Women and Pacifism'. Publications include: 'Landscapes, Seascapes and Dreamscapes of War: *Sigrid Storråda* (Valkyrie) by Selma Lagerlöf" in *Northern Atlantic Islands and the Sea: Seascapes and Dreamscapes,* (Cambridge Scholars Publishing, 2017).

Aya Shimano-Bardai is a sound artist and PhD researcher in the Musicology department of Sorbonne University/IReMus in Paris. She is currently writing her doctoral thesis on the development and aesthetics of sound art, in parallel to her artistic practice which combines electroacoustic composition and audiovisual works.

Ruairidh Tarvet (PhD, MA) is a tutor in Scandinavian Studies at the University of Edinburgh. His research interests include Scandinavian/German sociolinguistics, border studies, national minorities and nationalism. He is also a regular contributor to Danish and Scottish newspapers on issues relating to his research interests.

Dr Miriam Tveit (miriam.tveit@nord.no) is associate professor in medieval history at Nord University. Her main field of research is legal history in early- and High Medieval Europe, herein the legislation processes and legal politics, as well as the regulation of urban life and regional administration in northern Scandinavia.